VERGIL

VERGIL

A Biography

By
TENNEY FRANK

New York
RUSSELL & RUSSELL
1965

To

CORRIGENDA

Page 8,	line	19,	read	"Vergilius"
" 29,	"	25,	"	consensus
" 30,	footnote 1,		"	Velleius
" 38,	line	2,	"	naïveté
" 52,	"	22,	"	ὀργῆς
" 53,	"	1,	"	περί
" 57,	"	21,	"	necromantic
" 68,	"	18,	"	Syracosio
" 94,	"	17,	"	thoroughly
" 106,	"	15,	"	Zephyrique
" 113,	"	3,	"	monotonous
" 116,	"	14,	"	Theocritean
" 131,	"	16,	"	validas

PREFACE

MODERN literary criticism has accustomed us to interpret our masterpieces in the light of the author's daily experiences and the conditions of the society in which he lived. The personalities of very few ancient poets, however, can be realized, and this is perhaps the chief reason why their works seem to the average man so cold and remote. Vergil's age, with its terribly intense struggles, lies hidden behind the opaque mists of twenty centuries: by his very theory of art the poet has conscientiously drawn a veil between himself and his reader, and the scraps of information about him given us by the fourth century grammarian, Donatus, are inconsistent, at best unauthenticated, and generally irrelevant.

Indeed criticism has dealt hard with Donatus' life of Vergil. It has shown that the meager *Vita* is a conglomeration of a few chance facts set into a mass of later conjecture derived from a literal-minded interpretation of the *Eclogues,* to which there gathered during the credulous and neurotic decades of the second and third centuries an accretion of irresponsible gossip.

However, though we have had to reject many of the statements of Donatus, criticism has procured for us more than a fair compensation from another source. A series of detailed studies of the numerous minor poems attributed to Vergil by ancient authors and mediaeval manuscripts — till recently pronounced unauthentic by modern scholars — has compelled most of us to accept the *Appendix Vergiliana* at face value. These poems, written in Vergil's formative years before he had adopted the reserved manner of the classical style, are full of personal reminiscences. They reveal many important facts about his daily life, his occupations, his ambitions and his ideals, and best of all they disclose the processes by which the poet during an apprenticeship of ten years developed the mature art of the *Georgics* and the *Aeneid*. They have made it possible for us to visualize him with a vividness that is granted us in the case of no other Latin poet.

The reason for attempting a new biography of Vergil at the present time is therefore obvious. This essay, conceived with the purpose of centering attention upon the poet's actual life, has eschewed the larger task of literary criticism and has also avoided the subject of Vergil's literary sources — a theme to which scholars have generally devoted too much acumen. The book is therefore of brief compass, but it has been kept to its single theme in the conviction that the reader who will study Vergil's works as in some measure an outgrowth of the poet's own experiences will find a new meaning in not a few of their lines.

T. F.

CONTENTS

I

MANTUA DIVES AVIS

AMONG biographical commonplaces one frequently finds the generalization that it is the provincial who acquires the perspective requisite for a true estimate of a nation, and that it is the country-boy reared in lonely communion with himself who attains the deepest knowledge of human nature. If there be some degree of truth in this reflection, Publius Vergilius Maro, the farmer's boy from the Mantuan plain, was in so far favored at birth. It is the fifteenth of October, 70 B. C., that the Mantuans still hold in pious memory: in 1930 they will doubtless invite Italy and the devout of all nations to celebrate the twentieth centenary of the poet's birth.

Ancient biographers, little concerned with Mendelian speculation, have not reported from what stock his family sprang. Scientific curiosity and nationalistic egotism have compelled modern biographers to become anthropologists. Vergil has accordingly been referred, by some critic or other, to each of the several peoples that settled the Po Valley

4 VERGIL

in ancient times: the Umbrians, the Etruscans, the Celts, the Latins. The evidence cannot be mustered into a compelling conclusion, but it may be worth while to reject the improbable suppositions.

The name tells little. *Vergilius* is a good Italic *nomen* found in all parts of the peninsula,[1] but Latin names came as a matter of course with the gift of citizenship or of the Latin status, and Mantua with the rest of Cisalpine Gaul had received the Latin status nineteen years before Vergil's birth. The cognomen *Maro* is in origin a magistrate's title used by Etruscans and Umbrians, but *cognomina* were a recent fashion in the first century B.C. and were selected by parents of the middle classes largely by accident.

Vergil himself, a good antiquarian, assures us that in the *heroic* age Mantua was chiefly Etruscan with enclaves of two other peoples (presumably Umbrians and Venetians). In this he is doubtless following a fairly reliable tradition, accepted all the more willingly because of his intimacy with Maecenas, who was of course Etruscan:[2]

> Mantua dives avis, sed non genus omnibus unum,
> Gens illis triplex, populi sub gente quaterni,
> Ipsa caput populis; Tusco de sanguine vires.

[1] Braunholz, *The Nationality of Vergil, Classical Review*, 1915, 104 ff.
[2] *Aeneid*, X, 201–3.

Pliny seems to have supposed this passage a description of Mantua in Vergil's own day: Mantua Tuscorum trans Padum sola reliqua (III. 130). That could hardly have been Vergil's meaning, however; for the Celts who flooded the Po Valley four centuries before drove all before them except in the Venetian marshes and the Ligurian hills. They could not have left an Etruscan stronghold in the center of their path. Vergil was probably not Etruscan.

The case for a Celtic origin is equally improbable. From the time when the Senones burned Rome in 390 B. C. till Caesar conquered Gaul, the fear of invasions from this dread race never slumbered. During the weary years of the Punic war when Hannibal drew his fresh recruits from the Po Valley, the determination grew ever stronger that the Alps should become Rome's barrier line on the North. Accordingly the pacification of the Transpadane region continued with little intermission until Polybius [3] could say two generations before Vergil's birth that the Gauls had practically been driven out of the Po Valley, and that they then held but a few villages in the foothills of the Alps. If this be true, the open country of Mantua must have had but few survivors. And the few that

[3] Polybius, II. 35, 4 (written about 140 B. C.).

remained were not often likely to have the privilege of intermarrying with the Roman settlers who filled the vacuum. Romans were too proud of their citizenship to intermarry with *peregrini* and raise children who must by Roman laws forego the dignities of citizenship.[4]

A Celtic strain of romance has been from time to time claimed for Vergil's poetry, though those who employ such terms seldom agree in their definition of them. His romanticism may be more easily explained by his early devotion to the Catullan group of poets, and the Celtic traits — whatever they may be — by the close racial affiliations between Celts and Italians, vouched for by anthropologists. But the difficulty of applying the test of the " Celtic temperament " lies in the fact that there are apparently now no true representatives of the Celtic race from whom to establish a criterion. The peoples that have longest preserved dialects of the Celtic languages appear from anthropometric researches to contain a dominant strain of a different race, perhaps that of the pre-Indo-European inhabitants of Western Europe. It may be, therefore, that what Arnoldians now refer to the " Celts " is after all not Celtic. At best it is unsafe to search for racial

[4] Ulpian, *Dig.* V. 8, ex peregrino et cive Romano, peregrinus nascitur.

traits in the work of genius; in this instance it would but betray loose thinking.

The assumption of Celtic origin is, therefore, hazardous.[5] There is, however, a strong likelihood that Vergil's forbears were among the Roman and Latin colonists who went north in search of new homes during the second century B. C. Vergil's father was certainly a Roman citizen, for none but a citizen could have sent his son to Rome to prepare for a political career. Mantua indeed, a " Latin " town after 89 B. C., did not become a Roman municipality until after Vergil had left it, but Vergil's father, according to the eighth *Catalepton*, had earlier in his life lived in Cremona. That city was colonized by Roman citizens in 218 B. C. and recolonized in 190, and though the colonists were reduced to the " Latin status," the magistrates of the town and their descendants secured citizenship from the beginning, and finally in 89 B. C. the whole colony received full citizenship. But quite apart from this, all of Cisalpine Gaul, as the region was called, was receiving immigrants from all parts of Italy throughout the second century, when the fields farther south were being exhausted by long tilling,

[5] Vergil we know was tall and dark. The Gauls were as a rule fair with light hair. The Etruscans on the other hand, while dark, were generally short of stature. Such data are however not of great importance.

and were falling into the hands of capitalistic land-lords and grazers. Since Roman citizenship was a personal rather than a territorial right, such immigrants could preserve their political status despite their change of habitation. The probabilities are, therefore, that in any case Vergil, though born in the province, was of the old Latin stock.

About the child appropriate stories gathered in time, but what the biographers chose to repeat in the credulous days of Donatus, when Rome was almost an Oriental city, need not detain us long. To Donatus, no doubt, *Magia* seemed a suitable name for the mother of a poet who knew the mysteries of the lower world; that she dreamed prophetically of the coming greatness of her son, we may grant as a matter of course. Sober judgment, however, can hardly accept the miraculous poplar tree which shot up at the place of nativity, or the birth-stories deriving "Vergilus" from *virga*, contrary to early Latin nomenclature and phonology. It is well to mention these things merely so that we may keep in mind how little faith the late biographers really deserve.

Donatus is also inclined to accept the tradition that Vergil's father was a potter and a man of very humble circumstances. That Vergil's father made pottery may be true; a father's occupation was apt to be recorded in Augustan biography — but it requires some knowledge of Roman society to comprehend what these words meant at the end of the Republic. In Donatus' day a " potter " was a day-laborer in loin-cloth and leather apron, earning about twenty cents for a long day of fourteen hours. Needless to say, Vergil's leisured competence during many years did not draw from such a trickling source. Donatus had forgotten that in Vergil's day the economic system of Rome was entirely different. At the end of the Republic, the potters of Northern Italy conducted factories of enormous output, for they had with their artistic red-figured ware captured the markets of the whole Mediterranean basin. The actual workmen were not Roman citizens by any means, but slaves. And we should add that while industrial producers, like traders, were in general held in low esteem, because most of them were foreigners and freedmen, the producers of earthenware had by accident escaped from the general odium. The reason was simply that earthenware production began as a legitimate extension of agriculture — it was one form of turning the products of the villa-soil to the best use — and agriculture as we remember (including horticulture and stock-raising) continued into Cicero's day the only respectable income-bringing occupation in which a Roman senator could engage without apol-

ogy. That is the reason why even the names of
Cicero, Asinius Pollio, and Marcus Aurelius are to be
found on brick stamps when it would have been socially impossible for such men to own, shall we say,
hardware or clothing factories. Donatus was already
so far away from that day that he had no feeling for
its social tabus. The property of Vergil's father —
possibly a farm with a pottery on some part of it —
could hardly have been small when it supported the
young student for many years in his leisured existence at Rome and Naples under the masters that
attracted the aristocracy of the capital. The story of
Probus, otherwise not very reliable, may, therefore,
be true — that sixty soldiers received their allotments from the estates taken from Vergil's father.

Of no little significance is the fact that Vergil first
prepared himself for public life,[6] and progressed so
far as to accept one case in court. In order to enter
public life in those days it was customary to train
one's self as widely as possible in literature, history,
rhetoric, dialectic, and court procedure, and to attract
public notice for election purposes by taking a few
cases. It was not every citizen who dared enter such
a career. This was the one occupation that the nobility guarded most jealously. While any foreigner

[6] Donatus, 15; *Ciris*, 1.2; *Catal*. V.; Seneca, *Controv*. III.
praef. 8.

or freedman might become a doctor, banker, architect or merchant prince, he could not presume to stand up before a praetor to discuss the rights and wrongs of Roman citizens; and since the advocate's work was furthermore considered the legitimate preliminary to magisterial offices it must the more carefully be protected. It would have been quite useless for Vergil to prepare for this career had it been obviously closed. We have no sure record in Cicero's epoch of any young man rising successfully from the business or industrial classes to a career in public life except through the abnormal accidents provided by the civil wars. Presumably, therefore, Vergil's father belonged to a landholding family with some honors of municipal service to his credit.

Of the poet's physical traits we have no very satisfactory description or likeness. He was tall, dark and rawboned, retaining through life the appearance of a countryman, according to Donatus. He also suffered, says the same writer, the symptoms that accompany tuberculosis. The reliability of this rather inadequate description is supported by a second-century portrait of the poet done in a crude pavement mosaic which has been found in northern Africa.[7] To be sure the technique is so faulty that

[7] See *Monuments Piot.* 1897, pl. xx; *Atene e Roma*, 1913, opp. p. 191.

we cannot possibly consider this a faithful likeness. But we may at least say that the person represented — a man of perhaps forty-five — was tall and loose-jointed, and that his countenance, with its broad brow, penetrating eye, firm nose and generous mouth and chin, is distinctly represented as drawn and emaciated.

There is also an unidentified portrait in a half dozen mediocre replicas representing a man of twenty-five or thirty years which some archaeologists are inclined to consider a possible representation of Vergil.[8] It is the so-called " Brutus." The argument for its attribution deserves serious consideration. The bust, while it shows a far younger man than the African mosaic, reveals the same contour of countenance, of brow, nose, cheeks and chin. Furthermore it is difficult to think of any other Roman in private life who attained to such fame that six marble replicas of his portrait should have survived the omnivorous lime-kilns of the dark ages. The Barrocco museum of Rome has a very lifelike replica[9] of this type in half-relief. Though its firm, dry workmanship seems to be of a few decades

---

[8] See British School *Cat. of the Mus. Capitolino*, p. 355; Bernoulli, *Röm. Ikonographie*, I, 187, Helbig,[3] I, no. 872.

[9] Mrs. Strong, *Roman Sculpture* plate, CIX; Hekler, *Greek and Roman Portraits*, 188 a. The antiquity of this marble has been questioned.

later than Vergil's youth it may well be a fairly
faithful copy of one of the first busts of Vergil
made at the time when the *Eclogues* had spread his
fame through Rome.

A land of sound constitutions, mentally and phys-
ically, was the frontier region in which Vergil grew
to manhood; and had it not later been drained of its
sturdy citizenry by the civil wars and recolonized by
the wreckage of those wars it would have become
Italy's mainstay through the Empire. The earlier
Romans and Latins who had first accepted colonial
allotments or had migrated severally there for over
a century were of sterner stuff than the indolent
remnants that had drifted to the city's corn cribs.
These frontiersmen had come while the Italic stock
was still sound, not yet contaminated by the freedmen of Eastern extraction. Cities like Cremona and
Mantua were truer guardians of the puritanic ideals
of Cato's day than Rome itself. The clear expres-
sive diction of Catullus' lyrics, full of old-fashioned
turns, the sound social ideals of Vergil's *Georgics*,
the buoyant idealism of the *Aeneid* and of Livy's
annals speak the true language of these people. It
is not surprising then that in Vergil's youth it is a
group of fellow-provincials — returning sons of
Rome's former emigrants — that take the lead in
the new literary movements. They are vigorous,

clever young men, excellently educated, free from the city's binding traditionalism, well provided also, many of them, with worldly goods acquired in the new rich country. Such were Catullus of Verona, Varius Rufus, Quintilius Varus, Furius, and Alfenus of Cremona, Caecilius of Comum, Helvius Cinna apparently of Brescia, and Valerius Cato who somehow managed to inspire in so many of them a love for poetry.

II

SCHOOL AND WAR

To Cremona, Vergil was sent to school. Caesar, the governor of the province, was now conquering Gaul, and as Cremona was the foremost provincial colony from which Caesar could recruit legionaries, the school boys must have seen many a maniple march off to the battle-fields of Belgium. Those boys read their *Bellum Gallicum* in the first edition, serial publication. When we remember the devotion of Caesar's soldiers to their leader, we can hardly be surprised at the poet's lasting reverence for the great *imperator*. He must have seen the man himself, also, for Cremona was the principal point in the court circuit that Caesar traveled during the winters between his campaigns — whenever the Gauls gave him respite.

The *toga virilis* Vergil assumed at fifteen, the year that Pompey and Crassus entered upon their second consulship — a notice to all the world that the triumvirate had been continued upon terms that made Julius the arbiter of Rome's destinies.

That same year the boy left Cremona to finish his literary studies in Milan, a city which was now threatening to outstrip Cremona in importance and size. The continuation of his studies in the province instead of at Rome seems to have been fortunate: the spirit of the schools of the north was healthier. At Rome the undue insistence upon a practical education, despite Cicero's protests, was hurrying boys into classrooms of rhetoricians who were supposed to turn them into finished public men at an early age; it was assumed that a political career was every gentleman's business and that every young man of any pretensions must acquire the art of speaking effectively and of "thinking on his feet." The claims of pure literature, of philosophy, and of history were accorded too little attention, and the chief drill centered about the technique of declamatory prose. Not that the rhetorical study was itself made absolutely practical. The teachers unfortunately would spin the technical details thin and long to hold profitable students over several years. But their claims that they attained practical ends imposed on the parents, and the system of education suffered.

In the northern province, on the other hand, there was less demand for studies leading directly to the forum. Moreover, some of the best teachers were active there.[1] They were men of catholic tastes, who in their lectures on literature ranged widely over the

---

[1] Suetonius, *De Gram.* 3.

centuries of Greek masters from Homer to the latest popular poets of the Hellenistic period and over the Latin poets from Livius to Lucilius. Indeed, the young men trained at Cremona and Milan between the days of Sulla and Caesar were those who in due time passed on the torch of literary art at Rome, while the Roman youths were being enticed away into rhetoric. Vergil's remarkable catholicity of taste and his aversion to the cramping technique of the rhetorical course are probably to be explained in large measure, therefore, by his contact with the teachers of the provinces. Vergil did not scorn Apollonius because Homer was revered as the supreme master, and though the easy charm of Catullus taught him early to love the "new poetry," he appreciated none the less the rugged force of Ennius. Had his early training been received at Rome, where pedant was pitted against pedant, where every teacher was forced by rivalry into a partizan attitude, and all were compelled by material demands to provide a " practical education," even Vergil's poetic spirit might have been dulled.

How long Vergil remained at Milan we are not told; Donatus' *paulo post* is a relative term that might mean a few months or a few years. However, at the age of sixteen Vergil was doubtless ready for the rhetorical course, and it is possible that he went

to the great city as early as 54 B. C., the very year of
Catullus' death and of the publication of Lucretius'
De Rerum Natura. The brief biography of Vergil
contained in the Berne MS. — a document of doubtful value — mentions Epidius as Vergil's teacher in
rhetoric, and adds that Octavius, the future emperor,
was a fellow pupil. This is by no means unreasonable despite a difference of seven years in the ages of
the two pupils. Vergil coming from the provinces
entered rhetoric rather late in years, whereas Octavius must have required the aid of a master of
declamation early, since at the age of twelve he prepared to deliver the *laudatio funebris* at the grave
of his grandmother. Thus the two may have met
in Epidius' lecture room in the year 50 B. C. Vergil
could doubtless have afforded tuition under such a
master since he presently engaged the no less distinguished Siro. We have the independent testi-
mony of Suetonius that Epidius was Octavius' and
Mark Antony's teacher.

If Antony's style be a criterion, this new master of
Vergil's was a rhetorician of the elaborate Asianistic
style,[2] then still orthodox at Rome. This school —
except in so far as Cicero had criticized it for going
to extremes — had not yet been effectively chal-

---

[2] Octavius was drawn to the Atticistic principles by the
great master Apollodorus.

lenged by the rising generation of the chaster Atticists. Hortensius was still alive, and highly revered, and Cicero had recently written his elaborate *De Oratore* in which, with the apparent calmness of a still unquestioned authority, he laid down the program of the writer of ornate prose who conceived it as his chief duty to heed the claims of art. While not an out and out Asianist he advocates the claims of the " grand-style," so pleasing to senatorial audiences, with its well-balanced periods, carefully modulated, nobly phrased, precisely cadenced, and pronounced with dignity. To be sure, Calvus had already raised the banner of Atticism and had in several biting attacks shown what a simple, frugal and direct style could accomplish; Calidius, one of the first Roman pupils of the great Apollodorus, had already begun making campaign speeches in his neatly polished orations which painfully eschewed all show of ornament or passion; and Caesar himself, efficiency personified, had demonstrated that the leader of a democratic rabble must be a master of blunt phrases. But Calvus did not threaten to become a political force, Calidius was too even-tempered, and Caesar was now in the north, fighting with other weapons. Cicero's prestige still seemed unbroken. It was not till Caesar crossed the Rubicon in 49, after Hortensius had died, and Cicero

had been pushed aside as a futile statesman, that
Atticism gained predominance in the schools. Later,
in 46, Cicero in several remarkable essays again took
up the cudgels for an elaborate prose, but then his
cause was already lost. Caesar's victory had demonstrated that Rome desired deeds, not words.

When Virgil, therefore, turned to rhetoric, probably under Epidius, he received the training which
was still considered orthodox. His farewell[3] to
rhetoric — written probably in 48 — shows unmistakably the nature of the stuff on which he had been
fed. It is the bombast and the futile rules of the
Asianic creed against which he flings his unsparing
scazons.

> Begone ye useless paint-pots of the school;
> Your phrases reek, but not with Attic scent,
> Tarquitius' and Selius' and Varro's drool:
> A witless crew, with learning temulent.
> And ye begone, ye tinkling cymbals vain,
> That call the youths to drivelings insane.

Epidius, to be sure, is not mentioned, but we happen
to know that Varro — if this be the erudite friend of
Cicero — was devoted to the Asianic principles.
And Epidius, the teacher of the flowery Mark

---

[3] *Catalepton* V (Edition, Vollmer). Birt, *Jugendverse und
Heimatpoesie Vergils*, 1910, has provided a useful commentary
on the *Catalepton*.

Antony, may well be concealed in Vergil's list of
names even if mention of him was omitted for reasons of propriety.

This poem reveals the fact that Vergil did not,
like the young men of Cicero's youth, enjoy the
privilege of studying law, court procedure, and oratory by entering the law office, as it were, of some
distinguished senator and thus acquiring his craft
through observation, guided practice, and personal
instruction. That method, so charmingly described
by Cicero as in vogue in his youth, had almost passed
away. The school had taken its place with its mock
courts, contests in oratory, set themes in fictitious
controversies. The analytical rules of rhetoric were
growing ever more intricate and time-wasting, and
how pedantic they were even before Vergil's childhood may be seen by a glance into the anonymous
Auctor ad Herennium. The student had to know
the differences between the various kinds of cases,
demonstrativum, deliberativum and judiciale; he
must know the proportionate value to the orator of
inventio, dispositio, elocutio, memoria, and pronun-
tiatio, and how to manage each; he must know how
to apply inventio in each of the six divisions of the
speech: exordium, narratio, divisio, confirmatio, con-
futatio, conclusio. On the subject of adornment of
style a relatively small task lay in memorizing il-

lustrations of some sixty figures of speech — and so on ad infinitum. *Inane cymbalon juventutis* is indeed a fitting commentary on such memory tasks. The end of the poem cited betrays the fact that the poet had not been able to keep his attention upon his task. He had been writing verses; who would not?

Quite apart, however, from the unattractive content of the course, the gradual change in political life must have disclosed to the observant that the free exercise of talents in a public career could not continue long. The triumvirate was rapidly suppressing the free republic. Even in 52, when Pompey became sole consul, the trial of Milo was conducted under military guard, and no advocate dared speak freely. During the next two years every one saw that Caesar and Pompey must come to blows and that the resulting war could only lead to autocracy.

The crisis came in January of 49 B.C. when Vergil was twenty years old. Pompey with the consuls and most of the senators fled southward in dismay, and in sixty days, hotly pursued by Caesar, was forced to evacuate Italy. Caesar, eager to make short work of the war, to attack Spain and Africa while holding the Alpine passes and pressing in pursuit of Pompey, began to levy new recruits throughout Italy.[4] Vergil also seems to have been drawn in this draft,

---

[4] Cic. *Ad Att.* IX. 19, in March.

since this is apparently the circumstance mentioned in his thirteenth *Catalepton*. "Draft," however, may not be the right word, for we do not know whether Caesar at this time claimed the right to enforce the rules of conscription. In any case, it is clear from all of Vergil's references to Caesar that the great general always retained a strong hold upon his imagination. Like most youths who had beheld Caesar's work in the province close at hand, he was probably ready to respond to a general appeal for troops, and Labienus' words to Pompey on the battlefield of Pharsalia make it clear that Caesar's army was largely composed of Cisalpines. The accounting they gave of themselves at that battle is evidence enough of the spirit which pervaded Vergil's fellow provincials. Nor is it unlikely that Vergil himself took part, for one of the most poignant passages in all his work is the picture of the dead who lay strewn over the battlefield of Pharsalia.

It is also probable that Vergil had had some share in the cruises on the Adriatic conducted by Antony the summer and winter before Pharsalia. Not only does this poem speak of service on the seas, but his poems throughout reveal a remarkable acquaintance with Adriatic geography. If he took part in the work of that stormy winter's campaigns, when more than one fleet was wrecked, we can comprehend the intimate touches in the description of Aeneas' en-counters with the storms.

The thirteenth *Catalepton*, which mentions the poet's military service, is not pleasant reading. Written perhaps in 48 or 47 B.C., directed against some hated martinet of an officer, it bears various dis-agreeable traces of camp life, which was then not well-guarded by charitable organizations of every kind as now. We need quote only the first few lines:[5]

> You call me caitiff, say I cannot sail
> The seas again, and that I seem to quail
> Before the storms and summer's heat, nor dare
> The speeding victor's arms again to bear.

We know how frail Vergil's health was in later years. His constitution may well have been wrecked during the winter of 49 which Caesar himself, inured though he was to the storms of the North, found unusually severe. Vergil, it would seem from these lines, was given sick-leave and permitted to go back to his studies, though apparently taunted for not later returning to the army.

[5] Jacere me, quod alta non possim, putas
    Ut ante, vectari freta,
  Nec ferre durum frigus aut aestum pati
    Neque arma victoris sequi.

The verses were written before 46 B.C. when the *collegia compitalicia* were disbanded; Birt, *Rhein. Mus.* 1910, 348.

There is another brief epigram which — if we
are right in thinking Pompey the subject of the lines
— seems to date from Vergil's soldier days, the
third *Catalepton:*

> Aspice quem valido subnixum Gloria regno
>   Altius et caeli sedibus extulerat.
> Terrarum hic bello magnum concusserat orbem,
>   Hic reges Asiae fregerat, hic populos,
> Hic grave servitium tibi iam, tibi, Roma, ferebat
>   (Cetera namque viri cuspide conciderant),
> Cum subito in medio rerum certamine praeceps
>   Corruit, e patria pulsus in exilium.
> Tale deae numen, tali mortalia nutu
>   Fallax momento temporis hora dedit.[6]

Whether or not Pompey aspired to become autocrat at Rome, many of his supporters not only believed but desired that he should. Cicero, who did
not desire it, did, despite his devotion to his friend,
fear that Pompey would, if victorious, establish practically or virtually a monarchy.[7] Vergil, therefore,

----

[6] Behold one whom, upborne by mighty authority, Glory had
exalted even above the abodes of heaven. Earth's great orb had
he shaken in war, the kings and peoples of Asia had he broken,
grievous slavery was he bringing even to thee, O Rome, — for
all else had fallen before that man's sword, — when suddenly,
in the midst of his struggle for mastery, headlong he fell,
driven from fatherland into exile. Such is the will of Nemesis;
at a mere nod, in a moment of time, the faithless hour tricks
mortal endeavor.

[7] Cic. *Ad Att.* VIII, 11, 4; X, 4, 8.

if he wrote this when Pompey fled to Greece in 49, or after the rout at Pharsalia, was only giving expression to a conviction generally held among Caesar's officers. Quite Vergilian is the repression of the shout of victory. The poem recalls the words of Anchises on beholding the spirits of Julius and Pompey:

> Tuque prior, tu parce, genus qui ducis Olympo
> Proice tela manu, sanguis meus.

This is the poet's final conviction regarding the civil war in which he served; his first had not differed widely from this.

Vergil's one experience as advocate in the court room should perhaps be placed after his retirement from the army. Egit, says Donatus, et causam apud judices, unam omnino nec amplius quam semel. The reason for his lack of success Donatus gives in the words of Melissus, a critic who ought to know: in sermone tardissimum ac paene indocto similem. The poet himself seems to allude to his disappointing failure in the *Ciris:* expertum fallacis praemia volgi. How could he but fail? He never learned to cram his convictions into mere phrases, and his judgments into all-inclusive syllogisms. When he has done his best with human behavior, and the sentence is pronounced, he spoils the whole with a rebellious dis aliter visum. A successful advocate must know what not to see and feel, and he must have ready convictions at his tongue's end. In the *Aeneid* there are several fluent orators, but they are never Vergil's congenial characters.

III

THE "CULEX"

IT was apparently in the year 48 — Vergil was then twenty-one — that the poet attempted his first extended composition, the *Culex*, a poem that hardly deserved the honor of a versified translation at the hands of Spenser. This is indeed one of the strangest poems of Latin literature, an overwhelming burden of mythological and literary references saddled on the feeblest of fables.

A shepherd goes out one morning with his flocks to the woodland glades whose charms the poet describes at length in a rather imitative rhapsody. The shepherd then falls asleep; a serpent approaches and is about to strike him when a gnat, seeing the danger, stings him in time to save him. But — such is the fatalism of cynical fable-lore — the shepherd, still in a stupor, crushes the gnat that has saved his life. At night the gnat's ghost returns to rebuke the shepherd for his innocent ingratitude, and rather inappropriately remains to rehearse at great length the tale of what shades of old heroes he has seen in the lower regions. The poem contains 414 lines.

The *Culex* has been one of the standing puzzles of literary criticism, and would be interesting, if only to illustrate the inadequacy of stylistic criteria. Though it was accepted as Vergilian by Renaissance readers simply because the manuscripts of the poem and ancient writers, from Lucan and Statius to Martial and Suetonius, all attribute the work to him, recent critics have usually been skeptical or downright recusant. Some insist that it is a forgery or supposititious work; others that it is a liberally padded re-working of Vergil's original. Only a few have accepted it as a very youthful failure of Vergil's, or as an attempt of the poet to parody the then popular romances. Recent objections have not centered about metrical technique, diction, or details of style: these are now admitted to be Vergilian enough, or rather what might well have been Vergilian at the outset of his career. The chief criticism is directed against a want of proportion and an apparent lack of artistic sense betrayed in choosing so strange a character for the ponderous title-rôle. These are faults that Vergil later does not betray.

Nevertheless, Vergil seems to have written the poem. Its ascription to Vergil by so many authors of the early empire, as well as the concensus of the manuscripts, must be taken very seriously. But the internal evidence is even stronger. Octavius, to whom the poem is dedicated, is addressed *Octavi venerande* and *sancte puer*, a clear reference to the remarkable honor that Caesar secured for him by election to the office of pontiff [1] when he was approaching his fifteenth birthday and before he assumed the *toga virilis*. Vergil was then twenty-one years of age — nearing his twenty-second birthday — and we may perhaps assume in Donatus' attribution of the *Culex* to Vergil's sixteenth year a mistake in some early manuscript which changed the original XXI to XVI, a correction which the citations of Statius and Lucan favor.[2] Finally, when, as we shall see presently, Horace in his second *Epode*, accords Vergil the honor of imitating a passage of the *Culex*, Vergil returns the compliment in his *Georgics*. We have therefore not only Vergil's recognition of Horace's courtesy, but, in his acceptance of it, his acknowledgment of the *Culex* as his own.[3]

---

[1] Vellius, II. 59, 3, pontificatus sacerdotio *puerum* honoravit, that is, before he assumed the *toga virilis* on October 18th. Nicolaus Damascenus (4) confirms this. Octavius received the office made vacant by the death of Domitius at Pharsalia (Aug. 9). His birthday was Sept. 23, 63. This high office is the first indication that Caesar had chosen his grandnephew to be his possible successor. The boy was hardly known at Rome before this time. See *Classical Philology*, 1920, p. 26.

[2] Anderson, in *Classical Quarterly*, 1916, p. 225; and *Class. Phil.* 1920, p. 26. The dedicatory lines of the *Culex* imply that the body of the poem was already complete. Whether the interval was one of weeks or months or years the poet does not say. [3] *Classical Philology*, 1920, pp. 23, 33.

The *Culex,* therefore, is the work of a beginner addressed to a young lad just highly honored, but after all to a schoolboy whom Vergil had, presumably two years before, met in the lecture rooms of Epidius. Does this provide a key with which to unlock the hidden intentions of our strange treasure-trove of miscellaneous allusions? Let the reader remember the nature of the literary lectures of that day when dictionaries, reference books, and encyclopedias were not yet to be found in every library, and school texts were not yet provided with concise Allen and Greenough notes. The teacher alone could afford the voluminous "cribs" of Didymus. Roman schoolboys had not, like the Greeks, drunk in all myths by the easy process of nursery babble. By them the legends of Homer and Euripides must be acquired through painful schoolroom exegesis. Even the names of natural objects, like trees, birds, and beasts came into literature with their Greek names, which had to be explained to the Roman boys. Hence the teacher of literature at Rome must waste much time upon elucidating the text, telling the myths in full, and giving convenient compendia of metamorphoses, of Homeric heroes, of " trees and flowers of the poets," and the like. Epidius himself, a pedagogue of the progressive style, had doubtless proved an adept at this sort of thing. Claiming to be a descendant of an ancient hero who had one day transformed himself into a river-god, he must have had a knack for these tales. At any rate we are told that he wrote a book on metamorphosed trees.[4] When Octavius read the *Culex*, did he recognize in the quaint passage describing the shepherd's grove of metamorphosed trees (124–145) phrases from the lecture notes of their voluble teacher? Are there reminiscences lurking also in the long list of flowers so incongruously massed about the gnat's grave and in the two hundred lines that detail the ghostly census of Hades? If this is a parody at all, it is to remind Octavius of Epidian erudition. In any case it is a kind of prompter of the poetic allusions that occupied the boys' hours at school. The simple plot of the shepherd and the gnat was selected from the type of fable lore thought suitable for school-room reading. It served by its very incongruity as a suitable thread for a catalogue of facts and fiction. Vergil himself furnishes the clue for this interpretation of the *Culex*, but it has been overlooked because of the wretched condition of the text that we have. The first lines [5] of the poem seem to mean:

---

[4] Pliny, *Nat. Hist.* XVII. 243; Suetonius, *De Rhetoribus*, 4.
[5] Lines 3–5:

> lusimus (haec propter culicis sint carmina docta,
> omnis ut historiae per ludum consonet ordo
> notitiae) doctumque voces, licet invidus adsit.

" My verses on the *Culex* shall be filled with erudition so that all the lore of the past may be strung together playfully in the form of a story." That Martial considered it a boy's book appropriate for vacation hours between school tasks is apparent from the inscription: [6]

> Accipe facundi *Culicem*, studiose, Maronis,
> Ne nucibus positis, *Arma virumque* legas.

The *Culex* is then, after all, a poem of unique interest; it takes us into the Roman schoolroom to find at their lectures the two lads whose names come first in the honor roll of the golden age.

The poem is of course not a masterpiece, nor was it intended to be anything but a *tour de force*; but a comprehension of its purpose will at least save it from being judged by standards not applicable to it. It is not naïvely and unintentionally incongruous. To the modern reader it is dull because he has at hand far better compendia; it is uninspired no doubt: the theme did not lend itself to enthusiastic treatment; the obscurity and awkwardness of expression and the imitative phraseology betray a young unformed style. To analyze the art, however, would be to take the poem more seriously than Vergil intended it to be when he wrote currente calamo. Yet

[6] Martial, XIV. 185.

we may say that on the whole the modulation of the verse, the treatment of the caesural pauses [7] and the phrasing compare rather favorably with the Catullan hexameters which obviously served as its models, that in the best lines the poet shows himself sensitive to delicate effects, and that the pastoral scene — which Horace compliments a few years later — is, despite its imitative notes, written with enthusiasm, and reminds us pleasantly of the *Eclogues*.

[7] For stylistic and metrical studies of the *Culex*, see *The Caesura in Vergil*, Butcher, *Classical Quarterly*, 1914, p. 123; Hardie, *Journal of Philology*, XXXI, p. 266, and *Class Quart.* 1916, 32 ff.; Miss Jackson, *Ibid.* 1911, 163; Warde Fowler, *Class. Rev.* 1919, 96.

IV

THE "CIRIS"

IT was at about this same time, 48 B. C., that Vergil began to write the *Ciris*, a romantic epyllion which deserves far more attention than it has received, not only as an invaluable document for the history of the poet's early development, but as a poem possessing in some passages at least real artistic merit. The *Ciris* was not yet completed at the time when Vergil reached the momentous decision to go to Naples and study philosophy. He apparently laid it aside and did not return to it until he had been in Naples several years. It was not till later that he wrote the dedication. As we shall see, the author again laid the poem away, and it was not published till after his death. The preface written in Siro's garden is addressed to Messalla, who was a student at Athens in 45–4 B. C., and served in the republican army of Brutus and Cassius in 43–2. In it Vergil begs pardon for sending a poem of so trivial a nature at a time when his one ambition is to describe worthily the philosophic system that he has adopted. "Nevertheless," he says, "accept meanwhile this

poem: it is all that I can offer; upon it I have spent
the efforts of early youth. Long since the vow was
made, and now is fulfilled." (*Ciris*, 42–7.) [1]

The story, beginning at line 101, was familiar.
Minos, King of Crete, had laid siege to Megara,
whose king, Nisus, had been promised invincibility
by the oracles so long as his crimson lock remained
untouched. Scylla, the daughter of Nisus, however,
was driven by Juno to fall in love with Minos, her
father's enemy; and, to win his love, she yields to
the temptation of betraying her father to Minos.
The picture of the girl when she had decided to cut
the charmed lock of hair, groping her way in the
dark, tiptoe, faltering, rushing, terrified at the
fluttering of her own heart, is an interesting attempt
at intensive art: 209–219:

> cum furtim tacito descendens Scylla cubili
> auribus erectis nocturna silentia temptat
> et pressis tenuem singultibus aera captat.
> tum suspensa levans digitis vestigia primis
> egreditur ferroque manus armata bidenti
> evolat: at demptae subita in formidine vires
> caeruleas sua furta prius testantur ad umbras.
> nam qua se ad patrium tendebat semita limen,
> vestibulo in thalami paulum remoratur et alti
> suspicit ad gelidi nictantia sidera mundi
> non accepta piis promittens munera divis.

[1] On the question of authenticity, see, Class. Phil. 1920,
103 ff.

Her aged nurse, Carme, comes upon the bewildered
and shivering girl, folds her in her robe, and coaxes
the awful confession from her; 250–260:

> haec loquitur mollique ut se velavit amictu
> frigidulam iniecta circumdat veste puellam,
> quae prius in tenui steterat succincta crocota.
> dulcia deinde genis rorantibus oscula figens
> persequitur miserae causas exquirere tabis.
> nec tamen ante ullas patitur sibi reddere voces,
> marmoreum tremebunda pedem quam rettulit intra.
> illa autem " quid me " inquit, " nutricula, torques?
> quid tantum properas nostros novisse furores?
> non ego consueto mortalibus uror amore."

Scylla does not readily confess. The poet's charac-
terization of her as she protracts the story to avoid
the final confession reveals an ambitious though
somewhat unpracticed art. Carme tries in vain to
dissuade the girl, and must, to calm her, promise to
aid her if all other means fail. The aged woman's
tenderness for her foster child is very effectively
phrased in a style not without reminiscences of
Catullus (340–48):

> his ubi sollicitos animi relevaverat aestus
> vocibus et blanda pectus spe luserat aegrum,
> paulatim tremebunda genis obducere vestem
> virginis et placidam tenebris captare quietem
> inverso bibulum restinguens lumen olivo
> incipit ad crebros (que) insani pectoris ictus
> ferre manum assiduis mulcens praecordia palmis.
> noctem illam sic maesta super morientis alumnae
> frigidulos cubito subnixa pependit ocellos.

On the morrow the girl pleads with her father to make peace, with humorous naïvete argues with the counsellors of state, tries to bribe the seers, and finally resorts to magic. When nothing avails, she secures Carme's aid. The lock is cut, the city falls, the girl is captured by Minos — in true Alexandrian technique the catastrophe comes with terrible speed — and she is led, not to marriage, but to chains on the captor's galley. Her grief is expressed in a long soliloquy somewhat too reminiscent of Ariadne's lament in Catullus. Finally, Amphitrite in pity transforms the captive girl into a bird, the Ciris, and Zeus as a reward for his devout life releases Nisus, also transforming him into a bird of prey, and henceforth there has been eternal warfare between the Ciris and the Nisus:

> quacunque illa levem fugiens secat aethera pennis,
> ecce inimicus atrox magno stridore per auras
> insequitur Nisus; qua se fert Nisus ad auras,
> illa levem fugiens raptim secat aethera pennis.[1]

The *Ciris* with all its flaws is one of our best examples of the romantic verse tales made popular by the Alexandrian poets of Callimachus' school. The old legends had of course been told in epic or dramatic form, but changing society now cared less for the stirring action and bloodshed that had enter-

[1] These four lines occur again in the *Georgics*, I. 406-9.

tained the early Greeks. The times were ripe for a
retelling from a different point of view, with a more
patient analysis of the emotions, of the inner im-
pulses of the moment before the blow, the battle of
passions that preceded the final act. We notice also
in these new poems a preponderance of feminine
characters. These the masculine democracy of classical Athens had tended to disregard, but in the capi-
tals of the new Hellenistic monarchies, many influential and brilliant women rose to positions of
power in the society of the court. A poet would have
been dull not to respond to this influence. This new
note was of course one that would immediately appeal
to the Romans, for the ancient aristocracy, which had
always accorded woman a high place in society and
the home, had never died out at Rome. Indeed such
early dramatists as Ennius and Accius had already
felt the need of developing the interest of feminine
rôles when they paraphrased classical Greek plays for
their audiences. Thus both at Alexandria and at
Rome the new poets naturally chose the more romantic myths of the old regal period as fit for their
retelling.

But the search for a different interpretation and
a deeper content induced a new method of narration.
Indeed the stories themselves were too well known
to need a full rehearsal of the plot. Action might

frequently be assumed as known and relegated to a significant line or two here and there. The scenic setting, the individual traits of the heroes and heroines, their mental struggles, their silent doubts and hesitations, became the chief concern of the new poets. Horace called this the " purple-patch " method of writing.

The narrative devices, however, varied somewhat. Some poets discarded all idea of form. They roamed through the woods by any path that might appear. This is the way that Tibullus likes to treat a theme. Whatever semi-apposite topic happens to suggest itself, provided only it contains pleasing fancies, invites him to tarry a while; he may or may not bring you back to the starting point. Other poets still adhere to form, though the pattern must be elaborate enough to hide its scheme from the casual reader, and sufficiently elastic to provide space for sentiment and pathos. In his sixty-eighth poem Catullus employs what might be called a geometrical pattern, in fact a pyramid of un-equal steps. He mounts to the central theme by a series of verses and descends on the other side by a corresponding series. In the sixty-fourth poem, however, the *epyllion* which the author of the *Ciris* clearly had in mind, Catullus used an intricate but by no means balanced form. The poem opens with the sea voyage of Peleus on which he meets the sea-nymph, Thetis. Then the poet leaps over the interval to the marriage feast, only to dwell upon the sorrows of Ariadne depicted on the coverlet of the marriage couch; thence he takes us back to the causes of Ariadne's woes, thence forward to the vengeance upon Ariadne's faithless lover; then back to the second scene embroidered on the tapestry; and now finally to the wedding itself which ends with the Fates' wedding song celebrating the future glories of Peleus' promised son.

The *Ciris,* to be sure, is not quite so intricate, but here again we have only allusions to the essential parts of the story: how Scylla offended Juno, how she met Minos, how she cut the lock, and how the city was taken. We are not even told why Minos failed to keep his pledge to the maiden. In the midst of the tale, Carme suspends the action by a long reference to Minos' earlier passion for her own daughter, Britomartis, which caused the girl's destruction, but the lament in which this story is disclosed merely alludes to but does not tell the details of the story. The whole plot of the *Ciris* is in fact unravelled by means of a series af allusions and suggestions, exclamations and soliloquies, parentheses and aposiopeses, interrogations and apostrophes.

In verse-technique [2] the *Ciris* is as near Catullus'
Peleus and Thetis as it is the *Aeneid:* indeed it is as
reminiscent of the former as it is prophetic of the
latter. The spondaic ending which made the line
linger, usually over some word of emotional content,
(l. 158):

At levis ille deus, cui semper ad ulciscendum

was to Cicero the earmark of this style. The *Ciris* has
it less often than Catullus. Being somewhat unjustly
criticized as an artifice it was usually avoided in the
Aeneid. There are more harsh elisions in the *Ciris*
than in the poet's later work, reminding one again
of Catullan technique. In his use of caesuras Vergil
in the *Ciris* resembles Catullus: both to a certain extent distrust the trochaic pause. Its yielding quality,
however, brought it back into more favor in various
emotional passages of the *Aeneid;* but there it is
carefully modified by the introduction of masculine
stops before and after, a nuance which is hardly
sought after in the *Ciris* or in Catullus. Finally, the
sentence structure has not yet attained the mallea-

---

[2] See especially Skutsch, *Aus Vergils Frühzeit*, p. 74; Drachmann, *Hermes*, 1908, p. 412 ff.; L. G. Eldridge, *Num Culex
et Ciris*, etc. Giessen, 1914; Rand, *Harvard Studies*, XXX, p.
150. The introduction which was written last is more reminiscent of Lucretius. On the question of authenticity, see Drachmann, *loc. cit.* Vollmer, *Sitz. Bayer. Akad.* 1907, 335, and
Vergil's Apprenticeship, Class. Phil. 1920, p. 103.

bility of a later day. While the *Ciris*, like the *Peleus and Thetis*, is over-free with involved and parenthetical sentences, it has on the whole fewer runover lines so that indeed the frequent coincidence of sense pauses and verse endings almost borders on monotony.

These are but a few of the minor details that show Vergil in his youth a close reader of Catullus, and doubtless of Calvus, Cinna and Cornificius, who employed the same methods. It was from this group, not from Homer or Ennius, that Vergil learned his verse-technique. The exquisite finish of the *Aeneid* was the product of this technique meticulously reworked to the demands of an exacting poetic taste.

The *Ciris* gave Vergil his first lesson in serious poetic composition, and no task could have been set of more immediate value for the training of Rome's epic poet. In a national epic classical objectivity could not suffice for a people that had grown so self-conscious. Epic poetry must become more subjective at Rome or perish. To be sure the vices of the episodic style must be pruned away, and they were, mercilessly. The *Aeneid* has none of the meretricious involutions of plot, none of the puzzling half-uttered allusions to essential facts, none of the teasing interruptions of the neoteric story book. The poet also learned to avoid the danger of stressing trivial and impertinent pathos, and he rejected the elegancies of style that threatened to lead to preciosity. What he kept, however, was of permanent value. The new poetry, which had emerged from a society that was deeply interested in science, had taught Vergil to observe the details of nature with accuracy and an appreciation of their beauty. It had also taught him that in an age of sophistication the poet should not hide his personality wholly behind the veil. There is a pleasing self-consciousness in the poet's reflections — never too obtrusive — that reminds one of Catullus. It implies that poetry is recognized in its great rôle of a criticism of life. But most of all there is revealed in the *Ciris* an epic poet's first timid probing into the depths of human emotions, a striving to understand the riddles behind the impulsive body. One sees why Dido is not, like Apollonius' Medea, simply driven to passion by Cupid's arrow — the naïve Greek equivalent of the medieval love-philter — why Pallas' body is not merely laid on the funeral pyre with the traditional wailing, why Turnus does not meet his foe with an Homeric boast. That Vergil has penetrated a richer vein of sentiment, that he has learned to regard passion as something more than an accident, to sacrifice mere logic of form for fragments of vital emotion and flashes of new scenery, and finally that he enriched the Latin vocabulary with fecund words are in no small measure the effect of his early intensive work on the *Ciris* under the tutelage of Catullus.

Vergil apparently never published the *Ciris*, for he re-used its lines, indeed whole blocks of its lines with a freedom that cannot be paralleled. The much discussed line of the fourth *Eclogue:*

Cara deum suboles, magnum Jovis incrementum,

is from the *Ciris* (l. 398), so is the familiar verse of *Eclogue* VIII (l. 41):

Ut vidi, ut perii, ut me malus abstulit error,

and *Aeneid* II. 405:

Ad caelum tendens ardentia lumina frustra,

and the strange spondaic unelided line (*Aen.* III. 74):

Nereidum matri et Neptuno Aegaeo,

and a score of others. The only reasonable explanation [3] of this strange fact is that the *Ciris* had not been circulated, that its lines were still at the poet's disposal, and that he did not suppose the original would ever be published. The fact that the

[3] Drachmann, *Hermes*, 1908, p. 405.

process of re-using began even in the *Eclogues*[4] shows that he had decided to reject the poem as early as 41 B. C. A reasonable explanation is near at hand. Messalla, to whom the poem was dedicated, joined his lot with that of Mark Antony and Egypt after the battle of Philippi, and for Antony Vergil had no love. The poem lay neglected till he lost interest in a style of work that was passing out of fashion. Finding a more congenial form in the pastoral he sacrificed the *Ciris*.

[4] Especially in 8, 10, and 4. This method of re-working old lines reveals an extraordinary gift of memory in the poet, who so vividly retained in mind every line he had written that each might readily fall into the pattern of his new compositions without leaving a trace of the joining. Critics who have tried the task have been compelled to confess that the criterion of contextual appropriateness cannot alone determine whether or not these lines first occurred in the *Ciris*.

V

A STUDENT OF PHILOSOPHY
AT NAPLES

THE *Culex* seems to have been completed in
September 48 B. C., and the main part of the *Ciris*
was written not much later. Now came a crisis in
Vergil's affairs. Perhaps his own experience in the
law courts, or the conviction that public life could
contain no interest under an autocracy, or disgust at
rhetorical futility, or perhaps a copy of Lucretius
brought him to a stop. Lucretius he certainly had
been reading; of that the *Ciris* provides unmistakable
evidence. And the spell of that poet he never escaped. His farewell to Rome and rhetoric has been
quoted in part above. The end of the poem bids —
though more reluctantly — farewell to the muses
also:

> Ite hinc Camenae; vos quoque ite jam sane
> dulces Camenae (nam fatebimur verum,
> dulces fuistis): et tamen meas chartas
> revisitote, sed pudenter et raro.

It is to Siro that he now went, the Epicurean philosopher who, closely associated with the voluminous

Philodemus, was conducting a very popular garden-
school at Naples, outranking in fact the original
school at Athens. It is not unlikely that this is where
Lucretius himself had studied.

It is well to bear in mind that the ensuing years
of philosophical study were spent at Naples — a
Greek city then — and very largely among Greeks.
This fact provides a key to much of Vergil. Our
biographies have somehow assumed Rome as the
center of Siro's activities, though the evidence in
favor of Naples is unmistakable. Not only does
Vergil speak of a journey (Catal. V. 8):

> Nos ad beatos vela mittimus portus
> Magni petentes docta dicta Sironis,

and Servius say *Neapoli studuit,* and the *Ciris* mention *Cecropius hortulus,* and Cicero in all his references place Siro on the bay of Naples,[1] but a fragment of a Herculanean roll of Philodemus locates
the garden school in the suburbs of Naples.

Even after Siro's death — about 42 B. C. — Vergil seems to have remained at Naples, probably in-
heriting his teacher's villa. In 38 he with Varius
and Plotius came up from Naples to Sinuessa to

---

[1] *De Fin.* II. 119, Cumaean villa; *Acad.* II. 106, Bauli; *Ad.
Fam.* VI. 11.2; Vestorius is a Neapolitan; cf. *Class. Phil.* 1920,
p. 107, and *Am. Jour. Philology,* XLI, 115. For other possible references, see *Am. Jour. Phil.* 1920, XLI, 280 ff.

join Maecenas' party on their journey to Brundisium; Vergil wrote the *Georgics* at Naples in the thirties (*Georg.* IV. 460), and Donatus actually remarks that the poet was seldom seen at Rome.

As the charred fragments of Philodemus' rolls are published one by one, we begin to realize that the students of Vergil have failed to appreciate the influences which must have reached the young poet in these years of his life in a Greek city in daily communion with oriental philosophers like Philodemus and Siro. After the death of Phaedrus these men were doubtless the leaders of their sect; at least Asconius calls the former *illa aetate nobilissimus* (*In Pis.* 68). Cicero represents them as *homines doctissimos* as early as 60 B. C., and though in his tirade against Piso — ten years before Vergil's adhesion to the school — he must needs cast some slurs at Piso's teacher, he is careful to compliment both his learning and his poetry. Indeed there seems to be not a little direct use of Philodemus' works in Cicero's *De finibus* and the *De natura deorum* written many years later. In any case, at least Catullus, Horace, and Ovid made free to paraphrase some of his epigrams. And these verses may well guard us against assuming that the man who could draw to his lectures and companionship some of the brightest spirits of the day is adequately represented by the crabbed controversial essays that his library has produced. These essays follow a standard type and do not necessarily reveal the actual man. Even these, however, disclose a man not wholly confined to the *ipsa verba* of Epicurus, for they show more interest in rhetorical precepts than was displayed by the founder of the school; they are more sympathetic toward the average man's religion, and not a little concerned about the affairs of state. All this indicates a healthy reaction that more than one philosopher underwent in coming in contact with Roman men of the world, but it also doubtless reflects the tendencies of the Syrian branch of the school from which he sprang; for the Syrian group had had to cast off some of its traditional fanaticism and acquire a few social graces and a modicum of worldly wisdom in its long contact with the magnificent Seleucid court.

Philodemus was himself a native of Gadara, that unfortunate Macedonian colony just east of the Sea of Galilee, which was subjected to Jewish rule in the early youth of our philosopher. He studied with Zeno of Sidon, to whom Cicero also listened in 78, a masterful teacher whose followers and pupils, Demetrius, Phaedrus, Patro, probably also Siro, and of course Philodemus, captured a large part of the most influential Romans for the sect.[2]

[2] *Italiam totam occupaverunt.* Cic. *Tusc.* IV. 7.

How Philodemus taught his rich Roman patrons
and pupils to value not only his creed but the whole
line of masters from Epicurus we may learn from
the Herculanean villa where his own library was
found, for it contained a veritable museum of Epicurean worthies down to Zeno, perhaps not excluding
the teacher himself, if we could but identify his portrait.[3]

The list of influential Romans who joined the
sect during this period is remarkable, though of
course we have in our incidental references but a
small part of the whole number. Here belonged
Caesar, his father-in-law Piso, who was Philodemus'
patron, Manlius Torquatus, the consulars Hirtius,
Pansa, and Dolabella, Cassius the liberator, Tre-
batius the jurist, Atticus, Cicero's life-long friend,
Cicero's amusing correspondents Paetus and Gallus,
and many others. To some of these the attraction
lay perhaps in the philosophy of ease which excused
them from dangerous political labors for the en-
joyment of their villas on the Bay of Naples. But to
most Romans the greatest attraction of the doctrine
lay in its presentation of a tangible explanation of
the universe, weary as they were of a childish faith
and too practical-minded to have patience with metaphysical theories now long questioned and incompre-

[3] See *Class. Phil.* 1920, p. 113.

hensible except through a tedious application of dubious logic.

Vergil's companions in the *Cecropius hortulus*, destined to be his life-long friends, were, according to Probus, Quintilius Varus, the famous critic, Varius Rufus, the writer of epics and tragedies, and Plotius Tucca. Of his early friendship with Varius he has left a remembrance in *Catalepton* I and VII, with Varus in *Eclogue* VI. Horace combined all these names more than once in his verses.[4] That the four friends continued in intimate relationship with Philodemus, appears from fragments of the rolls.[5]

Of the general question of Philodemus' influence upon Varius and Vergil, Varus and Horace, the critics and poets who shaped the ideals of the Augustan literature, it is not yet time to speak. It will be difficult ever to decide how far these men drew their materials from the memories of their lecture-rooms; whether for instance Varius' *de morte* depended upon his teacher's περὶ θανάτου, as has been suggested, or to what extent Horace used the περὶ ὀργῆς and the περὶ κακιῶν when he wrote his

---

[4] Cf. Hor. *Sat.* i. 5.55; i. 10. 44–45 and 81; *Carm.* i. 24.

[5] *Rhein. Mus.*, 1890, p. 172. The names of Quintilius and Varius occur twice; the rest are too fragmentary to be certain, but the space calls for names of the length of Πλώ]τιε and Οὐ[εργίλιε and the constant companionship of these four men makes the restoration very probable.

first two epistles, or the περὶ κολακείας when he
instructed his young friend Lollius how to con-
duct himself at court, or whether it was this
teacher who first called attention to Bion, Neoptole-
mus, and Menippus; nor does it matter greatly,
since the value of these works lay rather in the art
of expression and timeliness of their doctrine than in
originality of view.

In the theory of poetic art there is in many respects
a marked difference between the classical ideals of
the Roman group and the rather luxurious verses of
Philodemus, but he too recognized the value of
restraint and simplicity, as some of his epigrams
show. Furthermore his theories of literary art are
frequently in accord with Horace's *Ars Poetica* on
the very points of chaste diction and precise expression which this Augustan group emphasized.   It
would not surprise his contemporaries if Horace re-
stated maxims of Philodemus when writing an essay
to the son and grandsons of Philodemus' patron.
However, after all is said, Vergil had questioned
some of the Alexandrian ideals of art before he came
under the influence of Philodemus, and the seventh
Catalepton gives a hint that Varius thought as Vergil. It is not unlikely that Quintilius Varus, Vergil's
elder friend and fellow-Transpadane, who had
grown up an intimate friend of Catullus and Calvus,

had in these matters a stronger influence than Philodemus.

There are, however, certain turns of sentiment in Vergil which betray a non-Roman flavor to one who comes to Vergil directly from a reading of Lucretius, Catullus, or Cicero's letters. This is especially true of the Oriental proskynesis found in the very first *Eclogue* and developed into complete "emperor worship" in the dedication of the *Georgics*. This language, here for the first time used by a Roman poet, is not to be explained as simple gratitude for great favors. It is not even satisfactorily accounted for by supposing that the young poet was somewhat slavishly following some Hellenistic model. Catullus had paraphrased the Alexandrian poets, but he could hardly have inserted a passage of this import. Nor was it mere flattery, for Vergil has shown in his frank praise of Cato, Brutus, and Pompey that he does not merely write at command. No, these passages in Vergil show the effects of the long years of association with Greeks and Orientals that had steeped his mind in expressions and sentiments which now seemed natural to him, though they must have surprised many a reader at Rome. His teachers at Naples had grown up in Syria and had furthermore carried with them the tradition of the Syrian branch of the school that had learned to adapt its language to suit the whims of the deified Seleucid monarchs. As Epicureans they also employed sacred names with little reverence. Was not Antiochus Epiphanes himself a " god," while as a member of the sect he belittled divinity?

Naples, too, was a Greek city always filled with Oriental trading folk, and these carried with them the language of subject races. It is at Pompeii that the earliest inscriptions on Italian soil have been found which recognize the imperial cult, and it is at Cumae that the best instance of a cult calendar has come to light. It is a note, one of the very few in the great poet's work, that grates upon us, but when he wrote as he did he was probably not aware that his years of residence in the " garden " had indeed accustomed his ear to some un-Roman sounds.[6] Octavian was of course not unaware of the advantage that accrued to the ruler through the Oriental theory of absolutism, and furtively accepted all such expressions. By the time Vergil wrote the *Aeneid* the Roman world had acquiesced, but then, to our surprise, Vergil ceases to accord divine attributes to Augustus.

Again, I would suggest that it was at Naples that

[6] Julius Caesar began as early as 45 B.C. to invite extraordinary honors for political purposes, but Roman literature seems not to have taken any cognizance of them at that time.

Vergil may most readily have come upon the " messianic " ideas that occur in the fourth *Eclogue,* for despite all the objections that have been raised against using that word, conceptions are found there which were not yet naturalized in the Occident. The child in question is thought of as a Soter whose *deeds* the poet hopes to sing (1. 54), and furthermore lines 7 and 50 contain unmistakably the Oriental idea of *naturam parturire,* as Suetonius phrases it (*Aug.* 94). Quite apart from the likelihood that the Gadarene may have gossiped at table about the messianic hopes of the Hebrews, which of course he knew, it is not conceivable that he never betrayed any knowledge of, or interest in, the prophetic ideas with which his native country teemed. Meleager, also a Gadarene, preserved memories of the people of his birthplace in his poems, and Caecilius of Caleacte, who seems to have been in Italy at about this time, was not beyond quoting Moses in his rhetorical works.[7]

Furthermore, Naples was the natural resort of all those Greek and Oriental rhetoricians and philosophers, historians, poets, actors, and artists who drifted Romeward from the crumbling courts of Alexandria, Antioch, and Pergamum. There they

[7] It is generally assumed that his book was the source for the quotation in *Pseudo-Longinus.*

could find congenial surroundings while discovering
wealthy patrons in the numerous villas of the idle
rich near by, and thither they withdrew at vacation
time if necessity called them to Rome for more
arduous tasks. Andronicus, the Syrian Epicurean,
brought to Rome by Sulla, made his home at nearby
Cumae; Archias, Cicero's client, also from Syria,
spent much time at Naples, and the poet Agathocles
lived there; Parthenius of Nicaea, to whom the
early Augustans were deeply indebted, taught Vergil at Naples. Other Orientals like Alexander, who
wrote the history of Syria and the Jews, and Tima-
genes, historian of the Diadochi, do not happen to
be reported from Naples, but we may safely assume
that most of them spent whatever leisure time they
could there.

Puteoli too was still the seaport town of Rome as
of all Central Italy, and the Syrians were then the
carriers of the Mediterranean trade.[8] That is one
reason why Apollo's oracles at Cumae and Hecate's
necromatic cave at Lake Avernus still prospered.
When Vergil explored that region, as the details of
the sixth book show he must have done, he had
occasion to learn more than mere geographic details.

That Vergil had Isaiah, chapter 11, before his
eyes when he wrote the fourth *Eclogue* is of course

---

[8] Frank, *An Economic History of Rome,* chap. xiv.

out of the question; there is not a single close
parallel of the kind that Vergil usually permits himself to borrow from his sources; we cannot even be
sure that he had seen any of the Sibylline oracles,
now found in the third book of the collection, which
contains so strange a syncretism of Mithraic, Greek,
and Jewish conceptions, but we can no longer doubt
that he was in a general way well informed and quite
thoroughly permeated with such mystical and apocalyptic sentiments as every Gadarene and any Greek
from the Orient might well know. It speaks well
for his love of Rome that despite these influences it
was he who produced the most thoroughly nationalistic epic ever written.

The first fruit of Vergil's studies in evolutionary
science at Naples was the *Aetna*, if indeed the poem
be his. The problem of the authorship has been
patiently studied, and the arguments for authenticity
concisely summarized by Vessereau [9] make a strong
case. The evidence is briefly this. Servius attributed the poem to Vergil in his preface and again
in his commentary on *Aeneid*, III, 578. Donatus
also seems to have done so, though some of our

[9] Vessereau, *Aetna*, xx ff; Rand, *Harvard Studies*, XXX, 106,
155 ff. It is difficult to avoid the conclusion that Seneca attributed the *Aetna* to Vergil in *ad Lucilium* 79, 5: The words
"Vergil's complete treatment" can hardly refer to the seven
meager lines found in the third book of the *Aeneid*.

manuscripts of his *Vita* contain the phrase *de qua ambigitur*. Again, the texts of the *Aetna* which we have agree also in this ascription. Internal evidence proves the poem to be a work of the period between 54 and 44, which admirably suits Vergilian claims. Its close dependence upon Lucretius gives the first date, its mention of the "Medea" of the artist Timomachus as being overseas, a work which was brought to Rome between 46 and 44, gives the second. Finally, the *Aetna* is by a student of Epicurean philosophy largely influenced by Lucretius. It would be difficult to make a stronger case short of a contemporaneous attribution. Has not Vergil himself referred to the *Aetna* in the preface of his *Ciris*, where he thanks the Muses for their aid in an abstruse poem (l. 93)?

Quare quae *cantus* meditanti mittere *caecos* [10]
Magna mihi cupido tribuistis praemia divae.

What other poem could he have had in mind? The designation does not fit the *Culex*, which is the only poem besides the *Aetna* that could be in question. It is best, therefore, to take the *Aetna* [11] into account

[10] Lucretius is very fond of using the word *caecus* with reference to abstruse and obscure philosophical and scientific subjects.

[11] When Vergil wrote the *Georgics*, on a subject which the poet of the *Aetna* derides as trivial (264–74) he seems to apologize for abandoning science in favor of a meaner theme, *Georgics* II, 483 ff. Is not this a reference to the *Aetna?*

in studying Vergil's life, even though we reserve a
place in our memories for that stray phrase *de qua
ambigitur*.

The poet after an invocation to Apollo justifies
himself for rejecting the favorite themes of myth
and fiction: the mysteries of nature are more worthy
of occupying the efforts of the mind. He has chosen
one out of very many that needs explanation. The
true cause of volcanic eruption, he says, is that air
is driven into the pores of the earth, and when this
comes into contact with lava and flint which contain
atoms of fire, it creates the explosions that cause such
destruction. After a second invitation to the reader
to appreciate the worth of such a theme he tells the
story of two brothers of Catania who, when other
refugees from Aetna's explosion rescued their
worldly goods, risked their lives to save their
parents.

The poem is not a happy experiment. There is
no lack of enthusiasm for the subject, despite the
fact that the science of that day was wholly inadequate to the theme. But Vergil could hardly realize
this, since both Stoics and Epicureans had adopted
the theory of the exploding winds. The real trouble
with the theme is its hopelessly prosaic ugliness.
Lucretius, by his imaginative power, had apparently
deceived him into thinking that any fragment of

science might be treated poetically. In his master
the "flaring atom streams" had attained the sub-
limity of a Platonic vision, and the very majestic
sadness of his materialism carried the young poet
off his feet. But the mechanism of Aetna remained
merely a puzzle with little to inspire awe, and the
theme contained inherently no deep meaning for humanity — which, after all, the scientific problem
must possess to lend itself to poetic treatment. The
poet indeed realized all this before he had finished.
He sought, with inadequate resources, to stir an emotion of awe in describing the eruption, to argue the
reader into his own enthusiasm for a scientific subject, to prove the humanistic worth of his problem
by asserting its anti-religious value, and finally, in a
Turneresque obtrusion of human beings, to tell the
story of the Catanian brothers. But though the
attempt does honor to his aesthetic judgment the
theme was incorrigible. Perhaps the recent erup-
tions of Aetna — they are reported for the years
50 and 46 B. C. — had given the theme a greater interest than it deserved. We may imagine how refugees from Catania had flocked to Naples and told
the tale of their suffering.

There is another element in the poem that is as
significant as it is prosaic, a spirit of carping at
poetic custom which reminds the reader of Philo-

demus' lectures. Philodemus, whether speaking of philosophy or music or poetry, always begins in the negative. He is not happy until he has soundly trounced his predecessors and opponents. The author of the *Aetna* has learned all too well this scholastic method, and his acerbity usually turns the reader away before he has reached the central theme. There is of course just a little of this tone left in the *Georgics* — Lucretius also has a touch of it — but the *Aeneid* has freed itself completely.

The compensation to the reader lies not so much in episodical myths, descriptions, and the story at the end, apologetically inserted on Lucretius' theory of sweetened medicine, as rather in the poet's contagious enthusiasm for his science, the thrill of discovery and the sense of wonder (l. 251):

> Divina est animi ac jucunda voluptas!

Men have wasted hours enough on trivialities (258):

> Torquemur miseri in parvis, terimurque labore.

A worthier occupation is science (274):

> Implendus sibi quisque bonis est artibus: illae
> Sunt animi fruges, haec rerum est optima merces.

And science must be worthy of man's divine majesty (224):

Non oculis solum pecudum miranda tueri
More nec effusis in humum grave pascere corpus;
Nosse fidem rerum dubiasque exquirere causas,
Ingenium sacrare caputque attollere caelo,
Scire quot et quae sint magno fatalia mundo
Principia.

This may be prose, but it has not a little of the magnificence of the Lucretian logic. The man who wrote this was at least a spiritual kinsman of Vergil.

VI

EPIGRAM AND EPIC

THE years of Vergil's sojourn in Naples were perhaps the most eventful in Rome's long history, and we may be sure that nothing but a frail constitution could have saved a man of his age for study through those years. After the battle of Pharsalia in 48, Caesar, aside from the lotus-months in Egypt, pacified the Eastern provinces, then in 46 subdued the senatorial remnants in Africa, driving Cato to his death, and in September of that year celebrated his fourfold triumph with a magnificence hitherto undreamed. All Italy went to see the spectacle, and doubtless Vergil too; for here it was, if we mistake not, that he first resolved to write an epic of Rome. The year 45 saw the defeat of the Pompeian remnants in Spain, and the first preparations for the great Parthian expedition which, as all knew, was to inaugurate the new Monarchy. Then came the sudden blow that struck Caesar down, the civil war that elevated Antony and Octavian and brought Cicero to his death, and finally the victory at Philippi which ended all hope of a republic. Through all this tur-

moil the philosophic group of the " Garden " continued its pursuit of science, commenting, as we shall
see, upon passing events.

The *Aetna* — which seems to date from about
47–6 — reveals the young philosopher, if it is Vergil, in a serious mood of single-minded devotion to
his new pursuit. But as may be inferred from the
fifth *Catalepton* he was not sure of not backsliding.
To the influence of Catullus, plainly visible all
through these brief poems, there was added the example of Philodemus who wrote epigrams from time
to time. Several of the *Catalepton* may belong to
this period. The very first,[1] addressed to Vergil's
lifelong friend Plotius Tucca, is an amusing trifle in
the very vein of Philodemus. The fourth, like the
first in elegiacs, is a gracious tribute to a departing
friend, Musa, perhaps his fellow-townsman Octavius
Musa.[2] It closes with a generous expression of unquestioning friendship that asks for no return:

> Quare illud satis est si te permittis amari
>   Nam contra ut sit amor mutuus, unde mihi?

---

[1] Dequa saepe tibi, venit?   sed, Tucca, videre
        Non licet.   Occulitur limine clausa viri.
    Dequa saepe tibi, non venit adhuc mihi; namque
        Si occulitur, longe est tangere quod nequeas.
    Venerit, audivi.   Sed iam mihi nuntius iste
        Quid prodest?   illi dicito cui rediit.

[2] See Horace, *Sat.* I. 10, 82; Servius on *Ecl.* IX. 7; Berne
Scholia on *Ecl.* VIII. 6.

That is the trait surely that accounts for Horace's outburst of admiration

> Animae quales neque candidiores
> Terra tulit.

The seventh is an epigram mildly twitting Varius for his insistence upon pure diction. The crusade for purity of speech had been given a new impetus a decade before by the Atticists, and we may here infer that Varius, the quondam friend of Catullus, was considered the guardian of that tradition. Vergil, despite his devotion to neat technique, may have had his misgivings about rules that in the end endanger the freedom of the poet. His early work ranged very widely in its experiments in style, and Horace's *Ars Poetica* written many years later shows that Vergil had to the very end been criticized by the extremists for taking liberties with the language. The epigram begins as though it were an erotic poem in the style of Philodemus. Then, having used the Greek word *pothos*, he checks himself as though dreading a frown from Varius, and substitutes the Latin word *puer*.

> Scilicet hoc sine fraude, Vari dulcissime, dicam:
> " Dispeream, nisi me perdidit iste pothos."
> Sin autem praecepta vetant me dicere, sane
> Non dicam, sed: " me perdidit iste puer."

For the comprehension of the personal allusions in the sixth and twelfth epigrams, we have as yet discovered no clue, and as they are trifles of no poetic value we may disregard them.

The fourteenth is, however, of very great interest. It purports to be a vow spoken before Venus' shrine at Sorrento pledging gifts of devotion in return for aid in composing the story of Trojan Aeneas.

Si mihi susceptum fuerit decurrere munus,
 O Paphon, o sedes quae colis Idalias,
Troius Aeneas Romana per oppida digno
 Iam tandem ut tecum carmine vectus eat:
Non ego ture modo aut picta tua templa tabella
 Ornabo et puris serta feram manibus —
Corniger hos aries humilis et maxima taurus
 Victima sacrato sparget honore focos
Marmoreusque tibi aut mille coloribus ales
 In morem picta stabit Amor pharetra.
Adsis o Cytherea: tuos te Caesar Olympo
 Et Surrentini litoris ara vocat.

The poem has hitherto been assigned to a period twenty years later. But surely this youthful ferment of hope and anxiety does not represent the composure of a man who has already published the *Georgics*. The eager offering of flowers and a many-hued statue of Cupid reminds one rather of the youth who in the *Ciris* begged for inspiration with hands full of lilies and hyacinths.

However, we are not entirely left to conjecture. There is indubitable evidence that Vergil began an epic at this time, some fifteen years before he published the *Georgics*. It seems clear also that the epic was an *Aeneid*, with Julius Caesar in the background, and that parts of the early epic were finally merged into the great work of his maturity. The question is of such importance to the study of Vergil's developing art that we may be justified in going fully into the evidence.[3] As it happens we are fortunate in having several references to this early effort. The ninth *Catalepton*, written in 42, mentions the poet's ambition to write a national poem worthy of a place among the great classics of Greece (l. 62):

> Si patrio Graios carmine adire sales.

The sixth *Eclogue* begins with an allusion to it:

> Prima Syracusio dignata est ludere versu
> Nostra, nec erubuit silvas habitare Thalia.
> Cum canerem reges et proelia, Cynthius aurem
> Vellit et admonuit, pastorem Tityre pinguis
> Pascere oportet oves, deductum dicere carmen.

This may be paraphrased: " My first song — the *Culex* — was a pastoral strain. When later I es-

---

[3] Cf. *Classical Quarterly*, 1920, 156.

sayed to sing of kings and battles, Phoebus warned
me to return to my shepherd song." On this passage Servius has the comment: significat aut Aenei-
dem aut gesta regum Albanorum. Donatus finally in
his *Vita* says explicitly: mox cum res Romanas in-
choasset, offensus materia, ad Bucolica transit. The
poem, therefore, was on the stocks before the
Bucolics. We may surmise that the death of Caesar,
whose deeds seem to have brought the idea of such
a poem to Vergil's mind, caused him to lay the work
aside.

Returning to the fourteenth *Catalepton*, we find
what seems to be a definite key to the date and circumstances of its writing. The closing lines are:

Adsis, o Cytherea: tuos te Caesar Olympo
Et Surrentini litoris ara vocat.

It was on September 26 in 46 B. C., that Julius
Caesar so strikingly called attention to his claims
of descent from Venus and Aeneas by dedicating
a temple to Venus Genetrix, the mother of the
Julian gens. It was on that day that Caesar " called
Venus from heaven " to dwell in her new temple.[4]

[4] Cassius Dio, 43, 22; Appian, II. 102. There is independent proof that *Catalepton* XIV is earlier than the *Georgics*.
In *Georgics* II, 146, Vergil repeats the phrase *maxima taurus
victima*, but the phrase must have had its origin in the *Catalepton*, since here *maxima* balances *humilis*. In the *Georgics*
the phrase is merely a verbal reminiscence, for there is nothing

Was not this the act that prompted the happy idea
of writing the epic of Aeneas? Vergil was then
living at Naples, and we can picture the poet fevered
with the new impulse, sailing away from his lectures
across the fair bay for a day's brooding. Could one
find a more fitting place than Venus's shrine at Sorrento for the invocation of the *Aeneid?*

How far this first attempt proceeded we shall
probably not know. Vergil's own words would imply that his early effort centered about Aeneas' wars
in Italy; the sixth *Eclogue,*

Cum canerem reges et proelia,

is rather explicit on this point. Furthermore, the erroneous reference of Calaeno's omen to Anchises in
the seventh book (l. 122) would indicate that this
part at least was written before the harpy-scene of
the third, for the latter is so extensive that the poet
could hardly have forgotten it if it had already been
written.

It is, however, in reading the first and fifth books
that I think we may profit most by keeping in mind
the fact that the poet had begun the *Aeneid* before
Caesar's death. In Book I, 286 ff., occurs a passage

---

in the context there to explain *maxima.* On the order of composition of the Aeneid, see M. M. Crump, *The Growth of the
Aeneid.*

which Servius referred to Julius Caesar. It reads:

Nascetur pulchra Troianus origine Caesar,
Imperium Oceano, famam qui terminet astris,
Iulius, a magno demissum nomen Iulo.
Hunc tu olim caelo, spoliis Orientis onustum,
Accipies secura; uocabitur hic quoque uotis.[5]

Very few modern editors have dared accept Servius'
judgment here, and yet if we may think of these
lines as adapted from (say) an original dedication to
Julius Caesar written about 45 B. C., the difficulties
of the commentators will vanish. The facts that
Vergil seems to have in mind are these: in September
46 B. C., Julius Caesar, after returning from
Thapsus, celebrated his four great triumphs over
Gaul, Egypt, Pontus, and Africa, displaying loads
of booty such as had never before been seen at Rome.
He then gave an extended series of athletic games,
of the kind described in Vergil's fifth book, including
a restoration of the ancient *ludus Troiae*. When
these were over he dedicated the temple of Venus
Genetrix, thereby publicly announcing his descent
from Venus, and presently proclaimed his own super-
human rank more explicitly by placing a statue of
himself among the gods on the Capitoline (Dio,
XLIII, 14–22). Are not the phrases, *imperium*

---

[5] The following lines (291–6) refer to the succeeding reign
of Augustus as the poet is careful to indicate in the words
tum positis-bellis.

Oceano and *spoliis Orientis onustum* a direct reference to this triumph which, of course, Vergil saw? And did not these dedications inspire the prophecy *uocabitur hic quoque uotis?* Be that as it may, it is difficult to refuse credence to Servius in this case, for Vergil here (I, 267–274 and 283) accepts Julius Caesar's claim of descent from Iulus, whereas in the sixth book, in speaking of the descent of the royal Roman line, he derives it, as was regularly done in Augustus' day, from Silvius the son of Aeneas and Lavinia (VI, 763 ff.). We must notice also that in the *Aeneid* as in the *Georgics* Augustus is regularly called ' Augustus Caesar ' or ' Caesar,' whereas in the only other references to Julius in the *Aeneid* the poet explicitly points to him by saying ' Caesar et omnis *Iuli* progenies' (VI, 789).

Servius, therefore, seems to be correct in regarding Julius as the subject of the passage in the first book, and it follows that the passage contains memories of the year 46 B. C., whether or not the lines were, as I suggest, first written soon after Caesar's triumph.

The fifth book also, despite the fact that its beginning and end show a late hand, contains much that can be best brought into connection with Vergil's earlier years. It is, for instance, easier to comprehend the poet's references to Memmius, Catiline, and Cluentius in the forties than twenty years later.

Vergil's strange comparison of Messalla to the *superbus Eryx* in *Catalepton* IX, written in 42 B. C.,[6] is also readily explained if we may assume that he has recently studied the Eryx myth in preparation for the contest of Book V (ll. 392–420). The poet's enthusiasm for the *ludus Troiae* is well understood as a description of what he saw at Caesar's re-introduction of the spectacle in 46. At Caesar's games Octavian, then sixteen years of age, must have led one of the troops:[7] in the fifth book Atys the ancestor of Octavian's maternal line led one column by the side of Iulus:

Alter Atys, genus unde Atii duxere Latini (l. 568).

Then, too, marks of youth pervade the substance of the book. The questionable witticisms might perhaps be attributed to an attempt to relieve the strain, but there is an unusual amount of Homeric imitation, and inartistic allusion to contemporaries which, as in the youthful *Bucolics*, destroys the dramatic illusion. Thus, Vergil not only dwells upon the ancestry of the Memmii, Sergii, and Cluentii, but insists upon reminding the reader of Catiline's conspiracy in the *Sergestus*, *furens animi* who dashes

[6] See Chapter VIII.
[7] The brief account of Nicolaus of Damascus (9) mentions that Octavius had charge of the Greek plays at the triumphal games.

upon the rock in his mad eagerness to win, and obtrudes etymology in the phrase *segnem Menoeten* (1. 173). One is tempted to suspect that the whole narrative of the boat-race is filled with pragmatic allusions. If the characters of his epic must be connected with well-known Roman families, it is at least interesting that the connections are indicated in the fifth book and not in the passages where the names first meet the reader. Does it not appear that the body of the book was composed long before the rest, and then left at the poet's death not quite furbished to the fastidious taste of a later day?

Finally, I would suggest that the strange and still unexplained [8] omen of Acestes' burning arrow in ll. 520 ff. probably refers to some event of importance to Segesta in the same year, 46 B. C. We are told by the author of the *Bellum Africanum* that Caesar mustered his troops for the African campaign at Lilybaeum in the winter of 47. We are not told that while there he ascended the mountain, offered sacrifices to Venus Erycina, and ordered his statue to be placed in her temple, or that he gave favors to the people of Segesta who had the care of that temple. But he probably did something of that kind, for as he had already vowed his temple to

[8] See however DeWitt, *The Arrow of Acestes*, Am. Jour. Phil. 1920, 369.

Venus Genetrix he could hardly have remained eight days at Lilybaeum so near the shrine of Aeneas' Venus without some act of filial devotion. If Vergil wrote any part of the fifth book in or soon after 46 this would seem to be the solution of the obscure passage in question.

It is of importance then in the study of the *Aeneid* to keep in mind the fact that the plot was probably shaped and many episodes blocked out while Vergil was young and Julius Caesar still the dominant figure in Rome. Many scenes besides those in the fifth book may find a new meaning in this suggestion. Does it not explain why so many traits in Dido's character irresistibly suggest Cleopatra,[9] why half the lines of the fourth book are reminiscent of Caesar's dallying in Egypt in 47? Do not the protracted battle scenes of the last book — otherwise so un-Vergilian — remind one of Caesar's never-ending campaigns against foes springing up in all quarters, and of the fact that Vergil had himself recently had a share in the struggle? The young Octavius, also, whose boyhood is so sympathetically sketched by Nicolaus (5-9) — a leader among his companions always, but ever devoted and generous — seems to peer through the portrait of Ascanius.[10] Vergil's

[9] Nettleship, *Ancient Lives of Virgil*, 104; Warde Fowler, *Religious Experience of the Roman People*, p. 415.

[10] See Warde Fowler, *The Death of Turnus*, pp. 87–92, on the character of Ascanius.

memories of the boy at school, the recipient of the *Culex*, the leader of the Trojan troop at Caesar's games, the lad of sixteen sitting for a day in the forum as *praefectus urbi*, seem very recent in the pages of the epic.

It would be futile to attempt to pick out definite lines and claim that these were parts of the youthful poem. Indeed the artistry of most of the verses discussed is, as any reader will notice, more on the plane of the later work than of the *Ciris*, written about 47–3 B. C. It is safe to say that Vergil did not in his youth write the sonorous lines of *Aen.* I, 285–290, just as they now stand. But as we may learn from the *Ciris*, which Vergil attempted to suppress, no poet has more successfully retouched lines written in youth and fitted them into mature work without leaving a trace of the process.

Critics have always expressed their admiration for the comprehensive scope of the *Aeneid*, its depth of learning, its finished artistry, and its wide range of observation. The substantial character of the poem is not a mystery to us when we consider how long its theme lay in the poet's mind.

VII

EPICUREAN POLITICS

CAESAR fell on the Ides of March, 44. The peaceful philosophic community at Herculaneum " seeking wisdom in daily intercourse " must have felt the shock as of an earthquake, despite Epicurean scorn for political ambition. Caesar had been friendly to the school; his father-in-law, Piso, had been Philodemus' life-long friend and patron, and, if we may believe Cicero, even at times a boon companion. Several of Caesar's nearest friends were Epicureans of the Neapolitan bay. Their future depended wholly upon Caesar. Dolabella was Antony's colleague in that year's consulship, while Hirtius and Pansa had been chosen consuls for the following year by Caesar. To add to the shock, the liberators had been led by a recent convert to the school, Cassius.

The community as a whole was Caesarian, a fact explained not wholly by Piso's relations to Philodemus and the friendly attitude of so many followers of Caesar, but also by the consideration that the leading spirits were Transpadanes: Vergil, Varius

and Quintilius, at least. But at Rome the political
struggle soon turned itself into a contest to decide
not whether Caesar's régime should be honored and
continued in the family — Octavius seemed at first
too young to be a decisive factor — but whether
Antony would be able to make himself Caesar's successor. When in July Brutus and Cassius were out-
manoeuvered by Antony, and Cicero fled helplessly
from Rome, it was Piso who stepped into the breach,
not to support Brutus and Cassius, but to check the
usurpation of Antony. This gave Cicero a program.
In September he entered the lists against Antony;
in December he accepted the support of Octavian
who had with astonishing daring for a youth of
eighteen collected a strong army of Caesar's veterans and placed himself at the service of Cicero and
the Senate in their warfare against Antony. Spring
found the new consuls, Hirtius and Pansa, both
Caesarians, with the aid of Octavian, Caesar's heir,
besieging Antony at the bidding of the Senate in
the defence of Decimus Brutus, one of Caesar's
murderers! Such was Cicero's skill in generalship.
Of course Caesarians were not wholly pleased with
this turn of events. Cicero's success would mean not
only the elimination of Antony — to which they did
not object—but also the recall of Brutus and Cassius,
and the consequent elimination of themselves from

political influence. Piso accordingly began to waver.
While assuring the Senate of his continued support
in their efforts to render Antony harmless, he re-
fused to follow Cicero's leadership in attempting the
complete restoration of Brutus' party. Cicero's
Philippics dwell with no little concern upon this
phase of the question.

We would expect the Garden group, friendly to
the memory of Caesar, to adopt the same point of
view as Piso and for the same reasons. They could
hardly have sympathized with the murderers of
Caesar. On the other hand, they had no reason for
supporting the usurpations of Antony, and seem to
have enjoyed Cicero's *Philippics* in so far as these
attacked Antony. Extreme measures were, however,
not agreeable to Epicureans, who in general had
nothing but condemnation for civil war. However,
Octavian's strong stand could only have pleased
them: Caesar's grand-nephew and heir would
naturally be to them a sympathetic figure.

A fragment of Philodemus, recently deciphered,[1]
reveals the teacher adopting in his lectures the very
point of view which we have already found in Piso.
The fragment is brief and mutilated, but so much is
clear: Philodemus criticizes the party of Cicero for
carrying the attack upon Antony to such extremes

[1] *Hermes,* 1918, p. 382.

that through fear of the liberators a reaction in
favor of Antony might set in. We find this
position reflected even in Vergil. He never speaks
harshly of the liberators, to be sure; in fact his indirect reference to Brutus in the *Aeneid* is remarkably sympathetic for an Augustan poet, but we have
two epigrams of his attacking partizans of Antony
in terms that remind us of passages in Cicero's
Philippics. It would almost appear that Vergil now
drew his themes for lampoons from Cicero's un-
forgettable phrases,[2] as Catullus had done some
fifteen years before. How thoroughly Vergil disliked Antony may be seen in the familiar line in
the *Aeneid* which Servius recognized as an allusion
to that usurper (*Aen.* VI. 622):

Fixit leges pretio atque refixit.

If Servius is correct, we have here again a reminder
of those stormy years. This, too, is a dagger drawn
from Cicero's armory. Again and again the orator
in the *Philippics* charges Antony with having used
Caesar's seal ring for lucrative forgeries in state
documents. It is interesting to find that Vergil's
school friend, Varius, in his poem on Caesar's death,

[2] Three other epigrams, VI, XII, XIII, have been assumed
by some critics to be direct attacks upon Antony, but the key to
them has been lost and certainty is no longer attainable.

called *De Morte*,[3] first put Cicero's charges into effective verse:

Vendidit hic Latium populis agrosque Quiritum
Eripuit: fixit leges pretio atque refixit.

The reference here, too, must have been to Antony. The circle was clearly in harmony in their political views.

The two creatures of Antony attacked by Cicero and Vergil alike are Ventidius and Annius Cimber. The epigram on the former takes the form of a parody of Catullus' " Phasellus ille," a poem which Vergil had good reason to remember, since Catullus' yacht had been towed up the Mincio past Vergil's home when he was a lad of about thirteen. Indeed we hope he was out fishing that day and shared his catch with the home-returning travelers. Parodies are usually not works of artistic importance, and this for all its epigrammatic neatness is no exception to the rule. But it is not without interest to catch the poet at play for a moment, and learn his opinion on a political character of some importance.

[3] Some recent critics have suggested that the poem may have been a general discussion of the fear of death, but Varius is constantly referred to as an epic poet (Horace, *Sat*. I. 10, 43; *Carm*. I. 6 and Porphyrio *ad loc*). His poem was written before Vergil's eighth *Eclogue* which we place in 41 B.C. (Macrobius, *Sat*. VI. 2. 20) and probably before the ninth (see 1.36).

Ventidius had had a checkered career. After captivity, possibly slavery and manumission, Caesar had found him keeping a line of post horses and pack mules for hire on the great Aemilian way, and had drafted him into his transport service during the Gallic War. He suddenly became an important man, and of course Caesar let him, as he let other chiefs of departments, profit by war contracts. It was the only way he could hold men of great ability on very small official salaries. Vergil had doubtless heard of the meteoric rise of this *mulio* even when he was at school, for the post-road for Caesar's great trains of supplies led through Cremona. After the war Caesar rewarded Ventidius further by letting him stand for magistracies and become a senator — which of course shocked the nobility. Muleteers in the Senate! The man changed his cognomen to be sure, called himself Sabinus on the election posters, but Vergil remembered what name he bore at Cremona. Caesar finally designated him for the judge's bench, as praetor, and this high office he entered in 43. He at once attached himself to Antony, who used him as an agent to buy the service of Caesarian veterans for his army. It was this that stirred Cicero's ire, and Cicero did not hesitate to expose the man's career. Vergil's lampoon is interesting then not only in its connections

with Catullus and the poet's own boyhood memories,
but for its reminiscences of Cicero's speeches and the
revelation of his own sympathies in the partizan
struggle. The poem of Catullus and Vergil's parody must be read side by side to reveal the purport
of Vergil's epigram.

Phaselus ille, quem videtis, hospites,
Ait fuisse navium celerrimus,
Neque ullius natantis impetum trabis
Nequisse praeterire, sive palmulis
Opus foret volare sive linteo.
Et hoc negat minacis Adriatici
Negare litus insulasve Cycladas
Rhodumque nobilem horridamque Thraciam
Propontida trucemve Ponticum sinum,
Ubi iste post phaselus antea fuit
Comata silva: nam Cytorio in iugo
Loquente saepe sibilum edidit coma.
Amastri Pontica et Cytore buxifer,
Tibi haec fuisse et esse cognitissima
Ait phaselus: ultima ex origine
Tuo stetisse dicit in cacumine,
Tuo imbuisse palmulas in aequore,
Et inde tot per inpotentia freta
Erum tulisse, laeva sive dextera
Vocaret aura, sive utrumque Iuppiter
Simul secundus incidisset in pedem;
Neque ulla vota litoralibus deis
Sibi esse facta, cum veniret a mari
Novissimo hunc ad usque limpidum lacum.
Sed haec prius fuere; nunc recondita
Senet quiete seque dedicat tibi,
Gemelle Castor et gemelle Castoris.

Vergil's parody,[4] which substitutes the mule-team plodding through the Gallic mire for Catullus' graceful yacht speeding home from Asia, follows the original phraseology with amusing fidelity:

> Sabinus ille, quem videtis, hospites
> Ait fuisse mulio celerrimus,
> Neque ullius volantis impetum cisi
> Nequisse praeterire, sive Mantuam
> Opus foret volare sive Brixiam.
> Et hoc negat Tryphonis aemuli domum
> Negare nobilem insulamve Caeruli,
> Ubi iste post Sabinus, ante Quinctio
> Bidente dicit attodisse forcipe
> Comata colla, ne Cytorio iugo
> Premente dura volnus ederet iuba.
> Cremona frigida et lutosa Gallia,
> Tibi haec fuisse et esse cognitissima
> Ait Sabinus: ultima ex origine
> Tua stetisse (dicit) in voragine,
> Tua in palude deposisse sarcinas
> Et inde tot per orbitosa milia
> Iugum tulisse, laeva sive dextera
> Strigare mula sive utrumque coeperat
>
> . . . .
>
> Neque ulla vota semitalibus deis
> Sibi esse facta praeter hoc novissimum,
> Paterna lora proximumque pectinem.
> Sed haec prius fuere: nunc eburnea
> Sedetque sede seque dedicat tibi,
> Gemelle Castor et gemelle Castoris.

[4] See *Classical Philology*, 1920, p. 114.

The other epigram referred to (*Catalepton II*) also attacks a creature of Antony's, Annius Cimber, a despised rhetorician who had been helped to high political office by Antony. Again Cicero's *Philippics* (XI.14) serve as our best guide for the background.

> Corinthiorum amator iste verborum,
> Iste iste rhetor, namque quatenus totus
> Thucydides, Britannus, Attice febris!
> Tau Gallicum min et sphin ut male illisit,
> Ita omnia ista verba miscuit fratri.

It might be paraphrased: "a maniac for archaic words, a rhetor indeed, he is as much and as little a Thucydides as he is a British prince, the bane of Attic style! It was a dose of archaic words and Celtic brogue, I fancy, that he concocted for his brother."

There seem to be three points of attack. Cimber, to judge from Cicero's invective, was suspected of having risen from servile parentage, and of trying, as freedmen then frequently did, to pass as a descendant of some unfortunate barbarian prince. Since his brogue was Celtic (*tau Gallicum*) he could readily make a plausible story of being British. Vergil seems to imply that the brogue as well as the name Cimber had been assumed to hide his Asiatic parentage. The second point seems to be that Cimber, though a teacher of rhetoric, was so ignorant of

Greek, that while proclaiming himself an Atticist, he used non-Attic forms and vaunted Thucydides instead of Lysias as the model of the simple style. Finally, it was rumored, and Cicero affects to believe the tale, that Cimber was not without guilt in the death of his brother. Vergil is, of course, not greatly concerned in deriding Atticism itself: to this school Vergil must have felt less aversion than to Antony's flowery style; it is the perversion of the doctrine that amuses the poet.

Taken in conjunction with other hints, these two poems show us where the poet's sympathies lay during those years of terror. There may well have been a number of similar epigrams directed at Antony himself, but if so they would of course have been destroyed during the reign of the triumvirate. Antony's vindictiveness knew no bounds, as Rome learned when Cicero was murdered.

VIII

LAST DAYS AT THE GARDEN

VERGIL's dedication of the *Ciris* to Valerius Messalla was, as the poem itself reveals, written several years after the main body of the poem. The most probable date is 43 B. C., when the young nobleman, then only about twenty-one, went with Cicero's blessing [1] to join Brutus and Cassius in their fight for the Republic. Messalla had then, besides making himself an adept at philosophy — at Naples perhaps, since Vergil knew him — and stealing away student hours at Athens for Greek verse writing, gained no little renown by taking a lawsuit against the most learned lawyer of the day, Servius Sulpicius. Cicero's letter of commendation, which we still have, is unusually laudatory.

The dedication of the *Ciris* reveals Vergil still eager to win his place as a rival of Lucretius. We may paraphrase it thus:

" Having tried in vain for the favor of the populace, I am now in the 'Garden' seeking a theme worthy of philosophy, though I have spent many years to other purpose. Now I have dared to ascend the mountain of wis-

[1] Cicero, *Ad Brutum*, I, 15.

dom where but few have ventured. Yet I must complete
these verses that I have begun so that the Muses may cease
to entice me further. Oh, if only wisdom, the mistress
of the four sages of old, would lead me to her tower
whence I might from afar view the errors of men; I
should not then honor one so great with a theme so trifling,
but I should weave a marvelous fabric like Athena's
pictured robe . . . a great poem on Nature, and into its
texture I should weave your name. But for that my powers
are still too frail. I can only offer these verses on which
I have spent many hours of my early school-days, a vow
long promised and now fulfilled."

It is apparent that the student still throbs with a
desire to become a poet of philosophy, and that he
is willing to appease the muses of lighter song only
because they insist on returning. But there is another
poem addressed to Messalla that is equally full of
personal interest.

Messalla, as we know from Plutarch's *Brutus,*
drawn partly from the young man's diary, joined
Cassius in Asia, and did noteworthy service in help-
ing his general win the Eastern provinces from the
Euxine to Syria for the Republican cause. Later
at Philippi he led the cavalry charge which broke
through the triumvirate line and captured Octavius'
camp. That was the famous first battle of Philippi,
prematurely reported in Italy as a decisive victory
for the Republican cause. Three weeks later the
forces clashed again and the triumvirs won a com-

plete victory. Messalla, who had been chosen commander by the defeated remnant, recognized the hopelessness of his position and surrendered to the victors.

Vergil's ninth *Catalepton* seems to have been written as a paean in honor of Messalla on receipt of the first incomplete report. The poem does not by any means imply that Vergil favored Brutus and Cassius or felt any ill-will towards Octavian. Vergil's regard for Messalla was clearly a personal matter, and of such a nature that political differences played no part in it. The poet's complete silence in the poem about Brutus and Cassius indicates that it is not to any extent the *cause* which interests him. Nor can a eulogy of a young republican at this time be considered as implying any ill-will toward Octavian, to whom Vergil was always devoted. At this early day Antony was still looked upon as the dominating person in the triumvirate, and for him Vergil had no love whatever. He may, therefore, though a Caesarian and friendly to Octavian, sing the praises of a personal friend who is fighting Antony's triumvirate.

The ninth *Catalepton*, like most eulogistic verse thrown off at high speed, has few good lines (indeed it was probably never finished), but it is exceedingly interesting as a document in Vergil's life.

Since it has generally been placed about fifteen years too late and therefore misunderstood, we must dwell at length on some of its significant details. The poem can be briefly summarized:

" A conqueror you come, the great glory of a mighty triumph, a victor on land and sea over barbarian tribes; and yet a poet too. Some of your verses have found a place in my pages, pastoral songs in which two shepherds lying under the spreading oak sing in honor of your heroine to whom the divinities bring gifts. The heroine of your song shall be more famous than the themes of Greek song, yes even than the Roman Lucrece for whose honor your sires drove the tyrants out of Rome.

" Great are the honors that Rome has bestowed upon the liberty-loving (Publicolas) Messallas for that and other deeds. So I need not sing of your recent exploits: how you left your home, your son, and the forum, to endure winter's chill and summer's heat in warfare on land and sea. And now you are off to Africa and Spain and beyond the seas.

" Such deeds are too great for my song. I shall be satisfied if I can but praise your verses."

The most significant passage is the implied comparison of Valerius Messalla with the founder of the Valerian family who had aided the first Brutus in establishing the republic as he now was aiding the last Brutus in restoring it. The comparison is the more startling because our Messalla later explicitly rejected all connection with the first Valerius and

seems never to have used the cognomen Publicola.
The explanation of Vergil's passage is obvious.[2] The
poet hearing of Messalla's remarkable exploit at
Philippi saw at once that his association with Brutus
would remind every Roman of the events of 509
B. C., and that the populace would as a matter of
course acclaim the young hero by the ancient cognomen "Publicola." Later, after his defeat and
submission, Messalla had of course to suppress every
indication that might connect him with "tyrannicide" stock or faction. The poem, therefore, must
have been written before Messalla's surrender in
42 B. C.

The poet's silences and hesitation in touching upon
this subject of civil war are significant of his mood.
The principals of the triumph receive not a word:
his friend is the "glory" of a triumph led by men
whose names are apparently not pleasant memories.
Nor is there any exultation over a presumed defeat
of "tyrants" and a restoration of a "republic."
The exploit of Messalla that Vergil especially
stresses is the defeat of "barbarians," naturally the
subjection of the Thracian and Pontic tribes and of
the Oriental provinces earlier in the year. And the
assumption is made (l. 51 ff.) that Messalla has, as

[2] The argument is given in full in *Classical Philology*, 1920,
p. 36.

a recognition of his generalship, been chosen to complete the war in Africa, Spain, and Britain. Most significant of all is Vergil's blunt confession that his mind is not wholly at ease concerning the theme (ll. 9–12): " I am indeed strangely at a loss for words, for I will confess that what has impelled me to write ought rather to have deterred me." Could he have been more explicit in explaining that Messalla's exploits, for which he has friendly praise, were performed in a cause of which his heart did not approve? And does not this explain why he gives so much space to Messalla's verses, and why he so quickly passes over the victory of Philippi with an assertion of his incapacity for doing it justice?

To the biographer, however, the passage praising Messalla's Greek pastorals is the most interesting for it reveals clearly how Vergil came to make the momentous decision of writing pastorals. Since Messalla's verses were in Greek they had, of course, been written two years before this while he was a student at Athens. Would that we knew this heroine upon whom he represents the divinities as bestowing gifts! Propertius, who acknowledged Messalla as his patron later employed this same motive of celestial adoration in honor of Cynthia (II. 3, 25), but surely Messalla's *herois* was, to judge from Vergil's comparison, a person of far higher station than Cynthia. Could she have been the lady he married upon his return from Athens? Such a treatment of a woman of social station would be in line with the customs of the " new poets," Catullus, Calvus, and Ticidas, rather than of the Augustans, Gallus, Propertius, and Tibullus. Vergil himself used the motive in the second *Eclogue* (l. 46), a reminiscence which, doubtless with many others that we are unable to trace, Messalla must have recognized as his own.

The pastoral which Vergil had translated from Messalla is quite fully described:

> Molliter hic *viridi patulae sub tegmine quercus*
>   Moeris pastores et Meliboeus erant,
> Dulcia jactantes alterno carmina versu
>   Qualia Trinacriae doctus amat iuvenis.

That is, of course, the very beginning of his own *Eclogues*. When he published them he placed at the very beginning the well-known line that recalled Messalla's own line:

> Tityre, tu *patulae recubans sub tegmine fagi.*

What can this mean but a graceful reminder to Messalla that it was he who had inspired the new effort? [3]

___

[3] Roman writers frequently observed the graceful custom of acknowledging their source of inspiration by weaving in

We may conclude then that Vergil's use of that line as the title of his *Eclogues* is a recognition of Messalla's influence.   Conversely it is proof, if proof were needed, that the ninth *Catalepton* is Vergil's.   We may then interpret line thirteen of the ninth *Catalepton:*

> pauca tua in nostras venerunt carmina chartas,

as a statement that in the autumn of 42, Vergil had already written some of his *Eclogues,* and that these early ones — presumably at least numbers II, III, and VII — contain suggestions from Messalla.

There was, of course, no triumph, and Vergil's eulogy was never sent, indeed it probably never was entirely completed.[4]   Messalla quickly made his peace with the triumvirs, and, preferring not to return to Rome in disgrace, cast his lot with Antony who remained in the East.   Vergil, who thorougly disliked Antony, must then have felt that for the present, at least, a barrier had been raised between him and Messalla.   Accordingly the *Ciris* also was abandoned and presently pillaged for other uses.

---

a recognizable phrase or line from the master into the very first sentence of a new work: cf. *Arma virumque cano* — Ἄνδρα μοι ἔννεπε (Lundström, *Eranos,* 1915, p. 4).   Shelley responding to the same impulse paraphrased Bion's opening lines in " I weep for Adonais — he is dead."

[4] It ought, therefore, not to be used seriously in discussions of Vergil's technique.

The news of Philippi was soon followed by orders
from Octavian — to be thoroughly accurate we
ought of course to call him Caesar — that lands
must now, according to past pledges, be procured in
Italy for nearly two hundred thousand veterans.
Every one knew that the cities that had favored the
liberators, and even those that had tried to preserve
their neutrality, would suffer. Vergil could, of
course, guess that lands in the Po Valley would be
in particular demand because of their fertility. The
first note of fear is found in his eighth *Catalepton:*

> Villula, quae Sironis eras, et pauper agelle,
>   Verum illi domino tu quoque divitiae,
> Me tibi et hos una mecum, quos semper amavi,
>   Si quid de patria tristius audiero,
> Commendo imprimisque patrem: tu nunc eris illi
>   Mantua quod fuerat quodque Cremona prius.

It is usually assumed from this passage that Siro
had recently died, probably, therefore, some time in
42 B. C., and that, in accordance with a custom frequently followed by Greek philosophers at Rome,
he had left his property to his favorite pupil. The
garden school, therefore, seems to have come to an
end, though possibly Philodemus may have continued it for the few remaining years of his life.
Siro's villa apparently proved attractive to Vergil,
for he made Naples his permanent home, despite

the gift of a house on the Esquiline from Maecenas.

This, however, is not Vergil's last mention of Siro, if we may believe Servius, who thinks that "Silenum" in the sixth *Eclogue* stands for "Sironem," its metrical equivalent. If, as seems wholly likely, Servius is right, the sixth *Eclogue* is a fervid tribute to a teacher who deserves not to be forgotten in the story of Vergil's education. The poem has been so strangely misinterpreted in recent years that it is time to follow out Servius' suggestion and see whether it does not lead to some conclusions.[5]

After an introduction to Varus the poem tells how two shepherds found Silenus off his guard, bound him, and demanded songs that he had long promised. The reader will recall, of course, how Plato also likened his teacher Socrates to Silenus. Silenus sang indeed till hills and valleys thrilled with the music: of creation of sun and moon, the world of living things, the golden age, and of the myths of Prometheus, Phaeton, Pasiphaë, and many others; he even sang of how Gallus had been captured by the Muses and been made a minister of Apollo.

A strange pastoral it has seemed to many! And

---

[5] Skutsch roused a storm of discussion over it by insisting that it was a catalogue of poems written by Gallus (*Aus Vergils Frühzeit.*) Cartault, *Étude sur les Bucoliques de Virgile* (p. 285), almost accepts Servius' suggestion: "un résumé de ses lectures et de ses études."

yet not so strange when we bear in mind that the
books of Philodemus reveal Vergil and Quintilius
Varus as fellow students at Naples. Surely Servius
has provided the key. The whole poem, with
its references to old myths, is merely a rehearsal of
schoolroom reminiscences, as might have been
guessed from the fine Lucretian rhythms with which
it begins:

> Namque canebat, uti magnum per inane coacta
> Semina terrarumque animaeque marisque fuissent
> Et liquidi simul ignis; ut his exordia primis
> Omnia et ipse tener mundi concreverit orbis;
> Tum durare solum et discludere Nerea ponto
> Coeperit, et rerum paulatim sumere formas;
> Iamque novum terrae stupeant lucescere solem.
> Altius atque ·cadant summotis nubibus imbres;
> Incipiant silvae cum primum surgere, cumque
> Rara per ignaros errent animalia montis.

The myths that follow are meant to continue this
list of subjects, only with somewhat less blunt ob-
viousness. They suggested to Varus the usual
Epicurean theories of perception, imagination, passion, and mental aberrations, subjects that Siro must
have discussed in some such way as Lucretius treated
them in his third and fourth books of the *De Rerum
Natura*.

It is, of course, not to be supposed that Siro had
lectured upon mythology as such. But the Epi-

curean teachers, despite their scorn for legends, employed them for pedagogical purposes in several ways. Lucretius, for instance, uses them sometimes for their picturesqueness, as in the *prooemium* and again in the allegory of the seasons (V. 732). He also employs them in a Euhemeristic fashion, explaining them as popular allegories of actual human experiences, citing the myths of Tantalus and Sisyphus, for example, as expressions of the ever-present dread of punishment for crimes. Indeed Vergil himself in the *Aetna* — if it be his — somewhat naïvely introduced the battle of the giants for its picturesque interest. It is only after he had enjoyed telling the story in full that he checked himself with the blunt remark:

(l. 74)   Haec est mendosae vulgata licentia famae.

Lucretius is little less amusing in his rejection of the Cybele myth, after a lovely passage of forty lines (II, 600) devoted to it.

Vergil was, therefore, on familiar ground when he tried to remind his schoolmate of Siro's philosophical themes by designating each of them by means of an appropriate myth. Perhaps we, who unlike Varus have not heard the original lectures, may not be able in every case to discover the theme from the myth, but the poet has at least set us out

on the right scent by making the first riddles very
easy. The *lapides Pyrrhae* (l. 41) refer of course
to the creation of man; *Saturnia regna* is, in Epicurean lore, the primitive life of the early savages;
furtum Promethei (l. 42) must refer to Epicurus'
explanation of how fire came from clashing trees
and from lightning. The story of Hylas (l. 43)
probably reminded Varus of Siro's lecture on images
and reflection, Pasiphaë (l. 46) of unruly passions,
explained perhaps as in Lucretius' fourth book,
Atalanta (l. 61) of greed, and Phaeton of ambition.
As for Scylla, Vergil had himself in the *Ciris* (l. 69)
mentioned, only to reject, the allegorical interpretation here presented, according to which she
portrays:

> " the sin of lustfulness
> and love's incontinence."

Vergil had not then met Siro, but he may have read
some of his lectures.

Finally, the strange lines on Cornelius Gallus
might find a ready explanation if we knew whether
or not Gallus had also been a member of the Neapolitan circle. Probus, if we may believe him, sug-
gests the possibility in calling him a schoolmate of
Vergil's, and a plausible interpretation of this eclogue
turns that possibility into a probability. The passage (ll. 64–73) may well be Vergil's way of re-

calling to Varus a well-beloved fellow-student who had left the circle to become a poet.

The whole poem, therefore, is a delightful commentary upon Vergil's life in Siro's garden, written probably after Siro had died, the school closed, and Varus gone off to war. The younger man's school days are now over; he had found his idiom in a poetic form to which Messalla's experiments had drawn him. The *Eclogues* are already appearing in rapid succession.

IX

MATERIALISM IN THE SERVICE OF POETRY

It has been remarked that Vergil's genius was of slow growth; he was twenty-eight before he wrote any verses that his mature judgment recognized as worthy of publication. A survey of his early life reveals some of the reasons for this tardy development. Born and schooled in a province he was naturally held back by lack of those contacts which stimulate boys of the city to rapid mental growth. The first few years at Rome were in some measure wasted upon a subject for which he had neither taste nor endowment. The banal rhetorical training might indeed have made a Lucan or a Juvenal out of him had he not finally revolted so decisively. However, this work at Rome proved not to be a total loss. His choice of a national theme for an epic and his insight into the true qualities of imperial Rome owe something to the study of political questions that his preparation for a public career had necessitated. He learned something in his Roman days that not even Epicurean scorn for politics could eradicate.

However, his next decision, to devote his life to philosophy, again retarded his poetic development. Certainly it held him in leash during the years of adolescent enthusiasms when he might have become a lyric poet of the neoteric school. A Catullus or a Keats must be caught early. Indeed the very dogmas of the Epicurean school, if taken in all earnestness, were suppressive of lyrical enthusiasm. The *Aetna* shows perhaps the worst effects of Epicurean doctrine in its scholastic insistence that myths must now give way to facts. Its author was still too absorbed in the microscopic analysis of a petty piece of research to catch the spirit of Lucretius who had found in the visions of the scientific workshop a majesty and beauty that partook of the essence of poetry.

In the end Vergil's poetry, like that of Lucretius, owed more to Epicureanism than modern critics — too often obsessed by a misapplied *odium philosophicum* — have been inclined to admit. It is all too easy to compare this philosophy with other systems, past and present, and to prove its science inadequate, its implications unethical, and its attitude towards art banal. But that is not a sound historical method of approach. The student of Vergil should rather remember how great was the need of that age for some practical philosophy capable of lifting the mind

out of the stupor in which a hybrid mythology had
left it, and how, when Platonic idealism had been
wrecked by the skeptics, and Stoicism with its hypo-
thetical premises had repelled many students, Epicurean positivism came as a saving gospel of en-
lightenment.

The system, despite its inadequate first answers,
employed a scientific method that gave the Romans
faith in many of its results, just at a time when
orthodox mythology had yielded before the first
critical inspection. As a preliminary system of illumination it proved invaluable. Untrained in
metaphysical processes of thought, ignorant of the
tools of exact science, the Romans had as yet been
granted no answers to their growing curiosity about
nature except those offered by a hopelessly naïve
faith. Stoicism had first been brought over by Greek
teachers as a possible guide, but the Roman, now
trained by his extraordinary career in world politics
to think in terms of experience, could have but little
patience with a metaphysical system that constantly
took refuge in a faith in aprioristic logic which had
already been successfully challenged by two centuries
of skeptics. The Epicurean at least kept his feet on
the ground, appealed to the practical man's faith in
his own senses, and plausibly propped his hypotheses
with analogous illustrations, oftentimes approaching

very close to the cogent methods of a new inductive
logic. He rested his case at least on the processes
of argumentation that the Roman daily applied in
the law-courts and the Senate, and not upon flights
of metaphysical reasoning. He came with a gospel of
illumination to a race eager for light, opening vistas
into an infinity of worlds marvelously created by
processes that the average man beheld in his daily
walks.

It was this capacity of the Epicurean philosophy
to free the imagination, to lift man out of a trivial
mythology into a world of infinite visions, and to
satisfy man's curiosity regarding the universe with
tangible answers [1] that especially attracted Romans
of Vergil's day to the new philosophy. Their experience was not unlike that of numberless men of
the last generation who first escaped from a puerile
cosmology by way of popularized versions of Dar-
winism which the experts condemned as unscientific.

Furthermore, Epicureanism provided a view of
nature which was apt in the minds of an imaginative
poet to lead toward romanticism. Stoicism indeed
pretended to be pantheistic, and Wordsworth has
demonstrated the value to romanticism of that atti-

---

[1] It is not quite accurate to say that the Romans made a
dogma of Epicurus' *ipse dixit* which destroyed scientific open-
mindedness. Vergil uses Posidonius and Zeno as freely as
the Stoic Seneca does Epicurus.

tude. But to the clear of vision Stoicism immediately took from nature with one hand what it had given with the other. Invariably, its rule of " follow nature " had to be defined in terms that proved its distrust of what the world called nature. As a matter of fact the Stoic had only scorn for naturalism. Physical man was to him a creature to be chained. Trust not the " scelerata pulpa; peccat et haec, peccat! " cries Persius in terror.

The earlier naïve animism of Greece and Rome had contained more of aesthetic value, for it was the very spring from which had flowed all the wealth of ancient myths. But the nymphs of that stream were dead, slain by philosophical questioning. The new poetic myth-making that still showed the influence of an old habit of mind was apt to be rather self-conscious and diffident, ending in something resembling the pathetic fallacy.

Epicureanism on the other hand by employing the theory of evolution was able to unite man and nature once more. And since man is so self-centered that his imagination refuses to extend sympathetic treatment to nature unless he can feel a vital bond of fellowship with it, the poetry of romance became possible only upon the discovery of that unity. This is doubtless why Lucretius, first of all the Romans, could in his prooemium bring back to nature that

sensuousness which through the songs of the trouba-
dours has become the central theme of romantic
poetry even to our day.

> Nam simulac species patefactast verna diei . . . —
> Aëriae primum volucres te diva tuumque
> Significant initum perculsae corda tua vi,
> Inde ferae pecudes persultant pabula laeta.

Vergil, convinced by the same philosophy, expresses
himself similarly:

> Et genus aequoreum, pecudes, pictaeque volucres
> amor omnibus idem.

And again:

> Avia tum resonant avibus virgulta canoris
> Et Venerem certis repetunt armenta diebus
> Parturit almus ager Zepherique trementibus auris
> Laxant arva sinus.

It is, of course, the theme of " Sumer is icumen in."
Lucretius feels so strongly the unity of naturally
evolved creation that he never hesitates to compare
men of various temperaments with animals of sundry
natures — the fiery lion, the cool-tempered ox —
and explain the differences in both by the same preponderance of some peculiar kind of " soul-atoms."

Obviously this was a system which, by enlarging
man's mental horizon and sympathies, could create
new values for aesthetic use. Like the crude evo-

lutionistic hypotheses in Rousseau's day, it gave one a more soundly based sympathy for one's fellows — since evolution was not yet " red in tooth and claw." If nature was to be trusted, why not man's nature? Why curse the body, any man's body, as the root-ground of sin?   Were not the instincts a part of man?   Might not the scientific view prove that the passions so far from being diseases, conditioned the very life and survival of the race?   Perhaps the evils of excess, called sin, were after all due to defects in social and political institutions that had applied incorrect regulative principles, or to the selfishly imposed religious fears which had driven the healthy instincts into tantrums.   Rid man of these erroneous fears and of a political system begot for purposes of exploitation and see whether by returning to an age of primitive innocence he cannot prove that nature is trustworthy.[2]

There is in this philosophy then a basis for a large humanitarianism, dangerous perhaps in its implications.   And yet it could hardly have been more perilous than the Roman orthodox religion which insisted only upon formal correctness, seldom upon ethical decorum, or than Stoicism with its categorical imperative, which could restrain only those who were already convinced.   The Stoic pretence of

[2] Lucretius, III, 37–93; II, 23–39; V, 1105–1135.

appealing to a natural law could be proved illogi-
cal at first examination, when driven to admit that
" nature " must be explained by a question-begging
definition before its rule could be applied.

Indeed the Romans of Vergil's day had not been
accustomed to look for ethical sanctions in religion
or creed.   Morality had always been for them a
matter of family custom, parental teaching of the
rules of decorum, legal doctrine regarding the uni-
versality of *aequitas*, and, more than they knew, of
puritanic instincts inherited from a well-sifted stock.
It probably did not occur to Lucretius and Vergil
to ask whether this new philosophy encouraged a
higher or a lower ethical standard.   Cicero, as statesman, does; but the question had doubtless come to
him first out of the literature of the Academy which
he was wont to read.   Despite their creed, Lucretius
and Vergil are indeed Rome's foremost apostles of
Righteousness; and if anyone had pressed home the
charge of possible moral weakness in their system
they might well have pointed to the exemplary life
of Epicurus and many of his followers.   To the
Romans this philosophy brought a creed of wide
sympathies with none of the " lust for sensation "
that accompanied its return in the days of Rousseau
and " Werther."   Had not the old Roman stock,
sound in marrow and clear of eye, been shattered by

wars and thinned out by emigration, only to be dis-
placed by a more nervous and impulsive people that
had come in by the slave trade, Roman civilization
would hardly have suffered from the application of
the doctrines of Epicurus.

Whether or not Vergil remained an Epicurean to
the end, we must, to be fair, give credit to that philosophy for much that is most poetical in his later
work, — a romantic charm in the treatment of nature, a deep comprehension of man's temper, a
broader sympathy with humanity and a clearer
understanding of the difference between social virtue and mere ritualistic correctness than was to be expected of a Roman at this time.

It is, however, very probable that Vergil remained
on the whole faithful to this creed [3] to the very end.
He was forty years of age and only eleven years
from his death when he published the *Georgics,*
which are permeated with the Epicurean view of
nature; and the restatement of this creed in the first
book of the *Aeneid* ought to warn us that his faith
in it did not die.

[3] This is, of course, not the view of Sellar, Conington,
Glover, and Norden, — to mention but a few of those who
hold that Vergil became a Stoic. See chapter XV for a
development of this view.

X

RECUBANS SUB TEGMINE FAGI

THE visitor to Arcadia should perhaps be urged to leave his microscope at home. Happiest, at any rate, is the reader of Vergil's pastorals who can take an unannotated pocket edition to his vacation retreat, forgetting what every inquisitive Donatus has conjectured about the possible hidden meanings that lie in them. But the biographer may not share that pleasure. The *Eclogues* were soon burdened with comments by critics who sought in them for the secrets of an early career hidden in the obscurity of an unannaled provincial life. In their eager search for data they forced every possible passage to yield some personal allusion, till the poems came to be nothing but a symbolic biography of the author. The modern student must delve into this material if only to clear away a little of the allegory that obscures the text.

It is well to admit honestly at once that modern criticism has no scientific method which can with absolute accuracy sift out all the falsehoods that obscure the truth in this matter, but at least a be-

ginning has been made in demonstrating that the
glosses are not themselves consistent. Those early
commentators who variously place the confiscation
of Vergil's farm after the battle of Mutina (43
B. C.), after Philippi (42) and after Actium (31),
who conceive of Mark Antony as a partizan of
Brutus, and Alfenus Varus as the governor of a
province that did not exist, may state some real facts:
they certainly hazard many futile guesses. The
safest way is to trust these records only when they
harmonize with the data provided by reliable historians, and to interpret the *Eclogues* primarily as
imaginative pastoral poetry, and not, except when
they demand it, as a personal record. We shall
here treat the *Bucolics* in what seems to be their
order of composition, not the order of their position
in the collection.

The eulogy of Messalla, written in 42 B. C., reveals Vergil already at work upon pastoral themes,
to which, as he tells us, Messalla's Greek eclogues
had called his attention. We may then at once reject the statement of the scholiasts that Vergil wrote
the *Eclogues* for the purpose of thanking Pollio,
Alfenus, and Gallus for having saved his estates
from confiscation. At least a full half of these
poems had been written before there was any material cause for gratitude, and, as we shall see presently,

these three men had in any case little to do with the matter. It will serve as a good antidote against the conjectures of the allegorizing school if we remember that these commentators of the Empire were for the most part Greek freedmen, themselves largely occupied in fawning upon their patrons. They apparently assumed that poets as a matter of course wrote what they did in order to please some patron — a questionable enough assumption regarding any Roman poetry composed before the Silver Age.

The second *Eclogue* is a very early study which, in the theme of the gift-bringing, seems to be reminiscent of Messalla's work.[1] The third and seventh are also generally accepted as early experiments in the more realistic forms of amoebean pastoral. Since the fifth, which should be placed early in 41 B. C., actually cites the second and third, we have a *terminus ante quem* for these two eclogues. To the early list the tenth should be added if it was addressed to Gallus while he was still doing military service in Greece, and with these we may place the sixth, discussed above.

The lack of realistic local color in these pastorals has frequently been criticized, on the supposition that Vergil wrote them while at home in Mantua,

[1] See Chapter VIII.

and ought, therefore, to have given true pictures of Mantuan scenery and characters. His home country was and is a montonous plain. The jutting crags with their athletic goats, the grottoes inviting melodious shepherds to neglect their flocks, the mountain glades and waterfalls of the *Eclogues* can of course not be Mantuan. The Po Valley was thickly settled, and its deep black soil intensively cultivated. A few sheep were, of course, kept to provide wool, but these were herded by farmers' boys in the orchards. The lone she-goat, indispensable to every Italian household, was doubtless tethered by a leg on the roadside. There were herds of swine where the old oak forests had not yet been cut, but the swine-herd is usually not reckoned among songsters. Nor was any poetry to be expected from the cowboys who managed the cattle ranches at the foot hills of the Alps and the buffalo herds along the undrained lowlands. Is Vergil's scenery then nothing but literary reminiscence?

In point of fact the pastoral scenery in Vergil is Neapolitan. The eighth *Catalepton* is proof that Vergil was at Naples when he heard of the dangers to his father's property in the North. It is doubtful whether Vergil ever again saw Mantua after leaving it for Cremona in his early boyhood. The property, of course, belonged not to him but to his father, who, as the brief poem indicates, had remained there with his family. The pastoral scenery seldom, except in the ninth *Eclogue,* pretends to be Mantuan. Even where, as in the first, the poem is intended to convey a personal expression of gratitude for Vergil's exemption from harsh evictions, the poet is very careful not to obtrude a picture of himself or his own circumstances. Tityrus is an old man, and a slave in a typical shepherd's country, such as could be seen every day in the mountains near Naples. And there were as many evictions near Naples as in the North. Indeed it is the Neapolitan country — as picturesque as any in Italy — that constantly comes to the reader's mind. We are told by Seneca that thousands of sheep fed upon the rough mountains behind Stabiae, and the clothier's hall and numerous fulleries of Pompeii remind us that wool-growing was an important industry of that region. Vergil's excursion to Sorrento was doubtless not the only visit across the bay. Behind Naples along the ridge of Posilipo,[2] below which Vergil was later buried, in the

[2] The picturesque road from Naples to Puteoli clung to the edge of the rocky promontory of Posilipo, finally piercing the outermost rock by means of a tunnel now misnamed the " grotto di Sejano." Most of the road is now under twenty feet of water: See Günther, *Pausilypon.* To see the splendid ridge as Vergil saw it from the road one must now row the length of it from Naples to Nésida, sketching in an abundance of ilexes and goats in place of the villas that now cover it.

mountains about Camaldoli, and behind Puteoli all
the way to Avernus — a country which the poet had
roamed with observant eyes — there could have been
nothing but shepherd country.   Here, then, are the
crags and waterfalls and grottoes that Vergil describes in the *Eclogues.*

And here, too, were doubtless as many melodious
shepherds as ever Theocritus found in Sicily, for
they were of the same race of people as the Sicilians.
Why should the slopes of Lactarius be less musical
than those of Aetna?   Indeed the reasonable reader
will find that, except for an occasional transference
of actual persons into Arcadian setting — by an allegorical turn invented before Vergil — there is no
serious confusion in the scenery or inconsistent treatment in the plots of Vergil's *Eclogues.*   But by failing to make this simple assumption — naturally due
any and every poet — readers of Vergil have need-
lessly marred the effect of some of his finest passages.

The fifth *Eclogue,* written probably in 41 B. C.,
is a very melodious Daphnis-song that has always
been a favorite with poets.   It has been and may be
read with entire pleasure as an elegy to Daphnis, the
patron god of singing shepherds.   Those, however,
who in Roman times knew Vergil's love of symbolism, suspected that a more personal interest led

him to compose this elegy. The death and apotheo-
sis of Julius Caesar is still thought by some to be
the real subject of the poem, while a few have accepted another ancient conjecture that Vergil here
wrote of his brother. The person mourned must,
however, have been of more importance than Vergil's brother. On the other hand, certain details in
the poem — the sorrow of the mother, for instance
— preclude the conjecture that it was Caesar, unless
the poet is here confusing his details more than we
need assume in any other eclogue.

It is indeed difficult to escape the very old persuasion that a sorrow so sympathetically expressed
must be more than a mere Theocritan reminiscence.
If we could find some poet — for Daphnis must be
that — near to Vergil himself, who met an unhappy
death in those days, a poet, too, who died in such
circumstances during the civil strife that general expression of grief had to be hidden behind a symbolic
veil, would not the poem thereby gain a theme
worthy of its grace? I think we have such a poet
in Cornificius, the dear friend of Catullus, to whom
in fact Catullus addressed what seem to be his last
verses.[3] Like so many of the new poets, Cornificius
had espoused Caesar's cause, but at the end was induced by Cicero to support Brutus against the trium-

[3] Catullus, 38.

virs. After Philippi Cornificius kept up the hope-
less struggle in Africa for several months until
finally he was defeated and put to death. If he be
Vergil's Daphnis we have an explanation of why
his identity escaped the notice of curious scholars.
Tactful silence became quite necessary at a time when
almost every household at Rome was rent by divided
sympathies, and yet brotherhood in art could hardly
be entirely stifled. From the point of view of the
masters of Rome, Cornificius had met a just doom as
a rebel. If his poet friends mourned for him it
must have been in some such guise as this.

In this instance the circumstantial evidence is
rather strong, for we are told by a commentator that
Valgius, an early friend of Vergil's, wrote elegies to
the memory of a " Codrus," identified by some as
Cornificius: [4]

> Codrusque ille canit quali tu voce canebas,
> Atque solet numeros dicere Cinna tuos.

That " shepherd " at least is an actual person, a
friend of Cinna, and a member of the neoteric
group; that indeed it is Cornificius is exceedingly
probable. The poet-patriot seems then not to have
been forgotten by his friends.

[4] *Scholia Veronensia*, Ecl. VII, 22. **The evidence** is presented in *Classical Review*, 1920, p. 49.

All too little is known about this friend of Catullus and Cinna, but what is known excites a keen interest. Though he was younger than Cicero by nearly a generation, the great orator [5] did him no little deference as a representative of the Atticistic group. In verse writing he was of Catullus' school, composing at least one epyllion, besides lyric verse. According to Macrobius, Vergil paid him the compliment of imitating him, and he in turn is cited by the scholiasts as authority for an opinion of Vergil's. If the Daphnis-song is an elegy written at his death — and it would be difficult to find a more fitting subject — the poem, undoubtedly one of the most charming of Vergil's *Eclogues*, was composed in 41 B. C. It were a pity if Vergil's prayer for the poet should after all not come true:

Semper honos, nomenque tuum laudesque manebunt.

The tenth *Eclogue*, to Gallus, steeped in all the literary associations of pastoral elegies, from the time of Theocritus' Daphnis to our own " Lycidas " and " Adonais," has perhaps surrounded itself with an atmosphere that should not be disturbed by biographical details. However, we must intrude. Vergil's associations with Gallus, as has been intimated, were those, apparently, of Neapolitan school days

[5] See Cicero's letter to him: *Ad Fam.* XII, 17, 2.

and of poetry. The sixth *Eclogue* delicately implies that the departure of Gallus from the circle
had made a very deep impression upon his teacher
and fellow students.

What would we not barter of all the sesquipeda-
lian epics of the Empire for a few pages written by
Cornelius Gallus, a thousand for each! This brilliant, hot-headed, over-grown boy, whom every one
loved, was very nearly Vergil's age. A Celt, as one
might conjecture from his career, he had met Octavius in the schoolroom, and won the boy's enduring admiration. Then, like Vergil, he seems to
have turned from rhetoric to philosophy, from
philosophy to poetry, and to poetry of the Catullan
romances, as a matter of course. It was Cytheris,
the fickle actress — if the scholiasts are right —
who opened his eyes to the fact that there were
themes for passionate poetry nearer home than the
legendary love-tales; and when she forgot him, finding excitement elsewhere during his months of service with Octavian, he nursed his morbid grief in un-
Roman self-pity, this first poet of the *poitrinaire*
school. His subsequent career was meteoric.
Octavian, fascinated by a brilliancy that hid a lack
of Roman steadiness, placed him in charge of the
stupendous task of organizing Egypt, a work that
would tax the powers of a Caesar. The romantic poet

lost his head. Wine-inspired orations that delighted his guests, portrait busts of himself in every town, grotesque catalogues of campaigns against unheard-of negro tribes inscribed even on the venerable pyramids did not accord with the traditions of Rome. Octavian cut his career short, and in deep chagrin Gallus committed suicide.

The tenth *Eclogue* [6] gives Vergil's impressions upon reading one of the elegies of Gallus which had apparently been written at some lonely army post in Greece after the news of Cytheris' desertion. In his elegy the poet had, it would seem, bemoaned the lot that had drawn him to the East away from his beloved. "Would that he might have been a simple shepherd like the Greeks about his tent, for their loves remained true!" And this is of course the very theme which Vergil dramatizes in pastoral form.

We, like Vergil, realize that Gallus invented a new genre in literature. He had daringly brought the grief of wounded love out of the realm of fiction — where classic tradition had insisted upon keeping it — into the immediate and personal song. The hint for this procedure had, of course, come from Catullus, but it was Gallus whom succeeding elegists all accredited with the discovery. Vergil at

---

[6] This is the interpretation of Leo, *Hermes*, 1902, p. 15.

once felt the compelling force of this adventuresome experiment. He gave it immediate recognition in his *Eclogues,* and Tibullus, Propertius, and Ovid became his followers.

The poems of Gallus, if the Arcadian setting is real, were probably written soon after Philippi. Vergil's *Eclogue* of recognition may have been composed not much later, for we have a right to assume that Vergil would have had one of the first copies of Gallus' poems. If this be true, the first and last few lines were fitted on later, when the whole book was published, to adapt the poem for its honorable position at the close of the volume.

XI

THE EVICTIONS

THE first and ninth *Eclogues,* and only these, concern the confiscations of land at Cremona and Mantua which threatened to deprive Vergil's father of his estates and consequently the poet of his income. There seems to be no way of deciding which is the earlier. Ancient commentators, following the order of precedence, interpreted the ninth as an indication of a second eviction, but there seems to be no sound reason for agreeing with them, since they are entirely too literal in their inferences. Conington sanely decides that only one eviction took place, and he places the ninth before the first in order of time. He may be right. The two poems at any rate belong to the early months of 41.

The obsequious scholiasts of the Empire have nowhere so thoroughly exposed their own mode of thought as in their interpretations of these two *Eclogues.* Knowing and caring little for the actual course of events, having no comprehension of the institutions of an earlier day, concerned only with extracting what is to them a dramatic story from the *Eclogues,* they put all the historical characters into impossible situations. The one thing of which they feel comfortably sure is that every *Eclogue* that mentions Pollio, Gallus and Alfenus Varus must have been a "bread and butter" poem written in gratitude for value received. Of the close literary associations of the time they seem to be unaware. To suit such purposes Pollio [1] is at times made governor of Cisalpine Gaul, and at times placed on the commission to colonize Cremona, Alfenus is made Pollio's "successor" in a province that does not exist, and Gallus is also made a colonial commissioner. If, however, we examine these statements in the light of facts provided by independent sources we shall find that the whole structure based upon the subjective inferences of the scholiasts falls to the ground.

We must first follow Pollio's career through this period. When the triumvirate was formed in 43, Pollio was made Antony's *legatus* in Cisalpine Gaul and promised the consulship for the year 40.[2] After Philippi, however, in the autumn of 42, Cisalpine Gaul was declared a part of Italy and, therefore, fell out of Pollio's control.[3] Nevertheless, he was not deprived of a command for the year remaining before his consulship (41 B. C.), but was permitted

[1] See Diehl, *Vitae Vergilianae*, pp. 51 ff.
[2] Appian, IV. 2 and V. 22.
[3] Appian, V. 3 and V. 22.

to withdraw to the upper end of the Adriatic with his
army of seven legions.[4] His duty was doubtless
to guard the low Venetian coast against the remnants
of the republican forces still on the high seas, and,
if he had time, to subdue the Illyrian tribes friendly
to the republican cause.[5] During this year, in which
Octavian had to besiege Lucius Antony at Perusia,
Pollio, a legatus of Mark Antony, was naturally not
on good terms with Octavian, and could hardly have
used any influence in behalf of Vergil or any one
else. After the Perusine war he joined Antony at
Brundisium in the spring of 40, and acted as his
spokesman at the conference which led to the
momentous treaty of peace. We may, therefore,
safely conclude that Pollio was neither governor nor
colonial commissioner in Cisalpine Gaul when
Cremona and Mantua were disturbed, nor could he
have been on such terms with Octavian as to use his
influence in behalf of Vergil. The eighth and fourth
Eclogues which do honor to him, seem to have nothing whatever to do with material favors. They
doubtless owe their origin to Pollio's position as a
poet, and Pollio's interest in young men of letters.

With regard to Alfenus and Gallus, the scholiasts
remained somewhat nearer the truth, for they had at

---

[4] Velleius Paterculus, II. 76.2; Macrobius, *Sat.* I. XI. 22.
[5] A task which he performed in 39.

hand a speech of Gallus criticizing the former for his behavior at Mantua. By quoting the precise words of this speech Servius [6] has provided us with a solid criterion for accepting what is consistent in the statements of Vergil's earlier biographers and eliminating some conjectures. The passage reads: " When ordered to leave unoccupied a district of three miles outside the city, you included within the district eight hundred paces of water which lies about the walls." The passage, of course, shows that Alfenus was a commissioner on the colonial board, as Servius says. It does not excuse Servius' error of making Alfenus Pollio's successor as provincial governor [7] after Cisalpine Gaul had become autonomous, nor does it imply that Alfenus had in any manner been generous to Vergil or to any one else. In fact it reveals Alfenus in the act of seizing an unreasonable amount of land. Vergil,[8] of course, recognizes Alfenus' position as commissioner in his ninth *Eclogue*, where he promises him great glory if he will show mercy to Mantua:

Vare, tuum nomen, superet modo Mantua nobis . . .

And Vergil's appeal to him was reasonable, since he,

[6] Servius *Dan.* on *Ecl.* IX. 10; ex oratione Cornelii in Alfenum. Cf. Kroll, in *Rhein. Museum,* 1909, 52.

[7] Servius *Dan.* on *Ecl.* VI. 6.

[8] Vergil, *Eclogue* IX, 26-29.

too, was a man of literary ambitions.[9] But there is
no proof that Alfenus gave ear to his plea; at any
rate the poet never mentions him again. Servius'
supposition that Alfenus had been of service to the
poet [10] seems to rest wholly on the mistaken idea that
the sixth *Eclogue* was obsequiously addressed to him.
As we have seen, however, Quintilius Varus has a
better claim to that poem.

The quotation from the speech of Gallus also
lends support to a statement in Servius that Gallus
had been assigned to the duty of exacting moneys
from cities which escaped confiscation.[11] For this
we are duly grateful. It indicates how Alfenus and
Gallus came into conflict since the latter's financial
sphere would naturally be invaded if the former
seized exempted territory for the extension of his
new colony of Cremona. In such conditions we can
realize that Gallus was, as a matter of course, interested in saving Mantua from confiscation, and
that in this effort he may well have appealed to
Octavian in Vergil's behalf. In fact his interpretation of the three-mile exemption might actually
have saved Vergil's properties, which seem to have
lain about that distance from the city.[12]

[9] See *Suffenus and Alfenus, Classical Quarterly,* 1920, p.
160.

[10] On *Eclogue* VI. 6.   [11] Servius *Dan.* on *Ecl.* VI. 64.

[12] *Vita Probiana, milia passuum XXX* is usually changed to
III on the basis of Donatus: *a Mantua non procul.*

Again, however, there is little reason for the supposition that Vergil's *Eclogues* in honor of Gallus have any reference whatever to this affair. The sixth followed the death of Siro, and the tenth seems to precede the days of colonial disturbances, if it has reference to Gallus as a soldier in Greece. If the sixth *Eclogue* refers to Siro, as Servius holds, then Vergil and Gallus had long been literary associates before the first and ninth were written.

The student of Vergil who has once compared the statements of the scholiasts with the historical facts at these few points, where they run parallel, will have little patience with the petty gossip which was elicited from the *Eclogues*. The story of Vergil's tiff with a soldier, for example, is apparently an inference from Menalcas' experience in *Eclogue* IX. 15; but " Menalcas " appears in four other *Eclogues* where he cannot be Vergil. The poet indeed was at Naples, as the eighth *Catalepton* proves. The estate in danger is not his, but that of his father, who presumably was the only man legally competent of action in case of eviction. Vergil's poem, to be sure, is a plea for Mantua, but it is clearly a plea for the whole town and not for his father alone. The landmark of the low hills and the beeches up to which the property was saved (IX.8) seems to be the limits of Mantua's boun-

daries, not of Vergil's estates on the low river-plains.
We need not then concern ourselves in a Vergilian
biography with the tale that Arrius or Clodius or
Claudius or Milienus Toro chased the poet into a
coal-bin or ducked him into the river.[13] The shepherds of the poem are typical characters made to
pass through the typical experiences of times of
distress.

The first *Eclogue, Tityre tu,* is even more general
than the ninth in its application. Though, of course,
it is meant to convey the poet's thanks to Octavian
for a favorable decree, it speaks for all the poor
peasants who have been saved. The aged slave,
Tityrus, does not represent Vergil's circumstances,
but rather those of the servile shepherd-tenants,[14] so
numerous in Italy at this time. Such men, though
renters, could not legally own property, since they
were slaves. But in practice they were allowed and
even encouraged to accumulate possessions in the
hope that they might some day buy their freedom,
and with freedom would naturally come citizenship
and the full ownership of their accumulations.
Many of the poor peasants scattered through Italy
were *coloni* of this type and they doubtless suffered
severely in the evictions. Tityrus is here pictured

[13] See Diehl, *Vitae Vergilianae,* p. 58.

[14] See Leo, *Hermes,* 1903, p. 1 ff, questioned by Stampini,
Le Bucoliche,[3] 1905, p. 93.

as going to the city to ask for his liberty, which would in turn ensure the right of ownership. Such is the allegory, simple and logical. It is only the old habit of confusing Tityrus with Vergil which has obscured the meaning of the poem. However, the real purpose of the poem lies in the second part where the poet expresses his sympathy for the luckless ones that are being driven from their homes; and that this represents a cry of the whole of Italy and not alone of his home town is evident from the fact that he sets the characters in typical shepherd country,[15] not in Mantuan scenery as in the ninth. The plaint of Meliboeus for those who must leave their homes to barbarians and migrate to Africa and Britain to begin life again is so poignant that one wonders in what mood Octavian read it. " En quo discordia cives produxit miseros! " was not very flattering to him.

The very deep sympathy of Vergil for the poor exiles rings also through the *Dirae*, a very surprising poem which he wrote at this same time, but on second thought suppressed. It has the bitterness of the first *Eclogue* without its grace and tactful beginning. The triumvirs were in no mood to read a book of lamentations. " Honey on the rim " was

---

[15] Capua and Nuceria were two of the cities near Naples where Vergil could see the work of eviction near at hand.

Lucretius' wise precept, and it was doubtless a prudent impulse that substituted the *Eclogue* for the "Curses." The former probably accomplished little enough, the latter would not even have been read.

The *Dirae* takes the form of a " cursing roundel," a form once employed by Callimachus, who may have inherited it from the East. It calls down heaven's wrath upon the confiscated lands in language as bitter as ever Mt. Ebal heard: fire and flood over the crops, blight upon the fruit, and pestilence upon the heartless barbarians who drive peaceful peasants into exile.

The setting is once more that of the country about Naples, of the Campanian hills and the sea coast, not that of Mantua.[16]   It is doubtless the miserable poor of Capua and Nuceria that Vergil particularly has in mind.   The singers are two slave-shepherds departing from the lands of a master who has been dispossessed.   The poem is pervaded by a strong note of pity for the lovers of peace, — " pii cives," shall we say the " pacifists," — who had been punished for refusing to enlist in a civil war.   A sympathy for them must have been deep in the gentle philosopher of the garden:

[16] It is just possible that " Lycurgus " (1. 8) who is spoken of as the author of the mischief is meant for Alfenus Varus, who boasted of his knowledge of law. Horace lampoons him as *Alfenus vafer.*

O male deuoti, praetorum crimina, agelli ! [17]
Tuque inimica pii semper discordia ciuis.
Exsul ego indemnatus egens mea rura reliqui,
Miles ut accipiat funesti praemia belli.
Hinc ego de tumulo mea rura nouissima uisam,
Hinc ibo in siluas: obstabunt iam mihi colles,
Obstabunt montes, campos audire licebit.[18]

For Vergil there was henceforth no joy in war or
the fruits of war. His devotion to Julius Caesar
had been unquestioned, and Octavian, when he
proved himself a worthy successor and established
peace, inherited that devotion. But for the patriots
who had fought the losing battle he had only a heart
full of pity.

Ne pueri ne tanta animis adsuescite bella,
Neu patriae validos in viscera vertite viris;
Tuque prior, tu parce, genus qui ducis Olympo,
Projice tela manu, sanguis meus!

[17] Ye fields accursèd for our statesmen's sins,
O Discord ever foe to men of peace,
In want, an exile, uncondemned, I yield
My lands, to pay the wages of a hell-born war.
Ere I go hence, one last look towards my fields,
Then to the woods I turn to close you out
From view, but ye shall hear my curses still.

[18] The *Lydia* which comes in the MS. attached to the
Dirae is not Vergil's. Nor can it be the famous poem of
that name written by Valerius Cato, despite the opinion
of Lindsay, *Class. Review*, 1918, p. 62. It is too slight and
ineffectual to be identified with that work. The poem abounds
with conceits that a neurotic and sentimental pupil of Propertius
— not too well practiced in verse writing — would be likely
to cull from his master.

XII

POLLIO

WE come finally to the two *Eclogues* addressed to Asinius Pollio. This remarkable man was only six years older than Vergil, but he was just old enough to become a member of Caesar's staff, an experience that matured men quickly. To Vergil he seemed to be a link with the last great generation of the Republic. That Catullus had mentioned him gracefully in a poem, and Cinna had written him a *propempticon*, that Caesar had spoken to him on the fateful night at the Rubicon, and that he had been one of Cicero's correspondents, placed him on a very high pedestal in the eyes of the studious poet still groping his way. It may well be that Gallus was the tie that connected Pollio and Vergil, for we find in a letter of Pollio's to Cicero that the former while campaigning in Spain was in the habit of exchanging literary chitchat with Gallus. That was in the spring of 43, at the very time doubtless when Pollio — as young men then did — spent his leisure moments between battles in writing tragedies. Vergil in his eighth *Eclogue*, perhaps with over-generous praise, compares these plays with those of Sophocles.

This *Eclogue* presents one of the most striking
studies in primitive custom that Latin poetry has
produced, a bit of realism suffused with a romantic
pastoral atmosphere.   The first shepherd's song is
of unrequited love cherished from boyhood for a
maiden who has now chosen a worthless rival.   The
second is a song sung while a deserted shepherdess
performs with scrupulous precision the magic rites
which are to bring her faithless lover back to her.
There are reminiscences of Theocritus of course, any
edition of the *Eclogues* will give them in full, but
Vergil, so long as he lived at Naples, did not have
to go to Sicilian books for these details.   He who
knows the social customs of Campania, the magical
charms scribbled on the walls of Pompeii, the deadly
curses scratched on enduring metal by forlorn lovers,
— curses hidden beneath the threshold or hearth-
stone of the rival to blight her cheeks and wrinkle
her silly face,— knows very well that such folks
are the very singers that Vergil might meet in his
walks about the hills of the golden bay.

The eighth *Eclogue* claims to have been written
at the invitation of Pollio, who had apparently
learned thus early that Vergil was a poet worth en-
couraging.   That the poem has nothing to do with
the confiscations, in so far at least as we are able to
understand the historical situation, has been sug-

gested above.   It is usually dated in the year of
Pollio's Albanian campaign in 39, that is a year after
his consulship.   Should it not rather be placed two
years earlier when Pollio had given up the Cisalpine
province and withdrawn to the upper Adriatic coast
preparatory to proceeding on Antony's orders against
the Illyrian rebels?   In the spring of 41 Pollio
camped near the Timavus, mentioned in line 6; two
years later the natural route for him to take from
Rome would be via Brundisium and Dyrrhachium.[1]
The point is of little interest except in so far as the
date of the poem aids us in tracing Pollio's influence
upon the poet, and in arranging the *Eclogues* in their
chronological sequence.

Finally,   we   have   the   famous   "Messianic"
Eclogue, the fourth, which was addressed to Pollio
during his consulship.   By its fortuitous resemblance
to the prophetic literature of the Bible, it came at one
time to be the best known poem in Latin, and elevated its author to the position of an arch-magician
in the medieval world.   Indeed, this poem was
largely influential in saving the rest of Vergil's works

---

[1] Antony's province did not extend beyond Scodra; the roads
down the Illyrian mountain from Trieste were not easy for
an army to travel; if the *Eclogues* were composed in three years
(Donatus) the year 39 is too late. Finally, Vellius, II, 76.2,
makes it plain that in 41 Pollio remained in Venetia contrary to
orders.   He had apparently been ordered to proceed into
Illyria at that time.

from the oblivion to which the dark ages consigned
at least nine-tenths of Latin literature.

The poem was written soon after the peace of
Brundisium — in the consummation of which Pollio
had had a large share — when all of Italy was exult-
ing in its escape from another impending civil war.
Its immediate purpose was to give adequate expression to this joy and hope at once in an abiding record
that the Romans and the rulers of Rome might read
and not forget. Its form seems to have been conditioned largely by a strange allegorical poem
written just before the peace by a still unknown poet.
The poet was Horace, who in the sixteenth epode
had candidly expressed the fears of Roman republi-
cans for Rome's capacity to survive. Horace had
boldly asked the question whether after all it was
not the duty of those who still loved liberty to aban-
don the land of endless warfare, and found a new
home in the far west — a land which still preserved
the simple virtues of the " Golden Age." Vergil's
enthusiasm for the new peace expresses itself as an
answer to Horace: [2] the " Golden Age " need not be
sought for elsewhere; in the new era of peace now
inaugurated by Octavian the Virgin Justice shall return to Italy and the Golden Age shall come to this

---

[2] Sellar, *Horace and the Elegiac Poets*, p. 123. Ramsay,
quoted by W. Warde Fowler, *Vergil's Messianic Eclogue*, p. 54.

generation on Italian soil. Vergil, however, introduces a new " messianic " element into the symbolism of his poem, for he measures the progress of the new era by the stages in the growth of a child who is destined finally to bring the prophecy to fulfillment. This happy idea may well have been suggested by table talks with Philodemus or Siro, who must at times have recalled stories of savior-princes that they had heard in their youth in the East. The oppressed Orient was full of prophetic utterances promising the return of independence and prosperity under the leadership of some long-hoped-for worthy prince of the tediously unworthy reigning dynasties. Indeed, since Philodemus grew to boyhood at Gadara under Jewish rule he could hardly have escaped the knowledge of the very definite Messianic hopes of the Hebrew people. It may well be, therefore, that a stray image whose ultimate source was none other than Isaiah came in this indirect fashion into Vergil's poem, and that the monks of the dark ages guessed better than they knew.

To attempt to identify Vergil's child with a definite person would be a futile effort to analyze poetic allegory. Contemporary readers doubtless supposed that since the Republic was dead, the successor to power after the death of Octavius and Antony would naturally be a son of one of these.

The settlements of the year were sealed by two marriages, that of Octavian to Scribonia and that of Octavian's sister to Antony. It was enough that some prince worthy of leadership could naturally be expected from these dynastic marriages, and that in either case it would be a child of Octavian's house.[3] Thus far his readers might let their imagination range; what actually happened afterwards through a series of evil fortunes has, of course, nothing to do with the question. Pollio is obviously addressed as the consul whose year marked the peace which all the world hoped and prayed would be lasting.

We have now reviewed the circumstances which called forth the *Eclogues*. They seem, as Donatus says, to have been written within a period of three years. The second, third, seventh and sixth apparently fall within the year 42, the tenth, fifth, eighth, ninth and first in the year 41, while the *Pollio* certainly belongs to the year 40, when Vergil became thirty years of age. The writing of these poems had called the poet more and more away from philosophy and brought him into closer touch with the sufferings and experiences of his own people. He had found a theme after his own heart, and with the theme had come a style and expression that fitted

[3] See *Class. Phil.* XI, 334.

his genius.   He abandoned Hellenistic conceits with their prettiness of sentiment, attained an easy modulation of line readily responding to a variety of emotions, learned the dignity of his own language as he acquired a deeper sympathy for the sufferings of his own people.   There is a new note, as there is a new rhythm in:

Magnus ab integro saeclorum nascitur ordo.

XIII

THE CIRCLE OF MAECENAS

JULIUS CAESAR had learned from bitter experience that poets were dangerous enemies. Cicero's innuendoes were disagreeable enough but they might be forgotten. When, however, Catullus and Calvus put them into biting epigrams there was no forgetting. This was doubtless Caesar's chief reason for his constant endeavor to win the goodwill of the young poets, and he ultimately did win that of Calvus and Catullus. Whether Octavian, and his sage adviser Maecenas, acted from the same motive we do not know, though they too had seen in Vergil's epigrams on Antony's creatures, and in Horace's sixteenth epode that the poets of the new generation seemed likely to give effective expression to political sentiments. At any rate, the new court at Rome began very soon to make generous overtures to the literary men of the day.

Pollio, Octavian's senior by many years, and of noble family, could hardly be approached. Though gradually drawing away from Antony, he had so closely associated himself with this brilliant companion of his Gallic-war days, that he preferred not to take a subordinate place at the Roman court. Messalla, who had entered the service of Antony, was also out of reach. There remained the brilliant circle of young men at Naples, men whose names occurred in the dedications of Philodemus' lectures: Vergil, Varius, Plotius and Quintilius Varus, three of whom at least were from the north and would naturally be inclined to look upon Octavian with sympathy.

Varius had already written his epic *De Morte* which seems to have mourned Caesar's death, and, though in hidden language, he had alluded bitterly to Antony's usurpations in the year that followed the murder. Before Vergil's epic appeared it was Varius who was always considered the epic poet of the group. Of Plotius Tucca we know little except that he is called a poet, was a constant member of the circle, and with Varius the literary executor who published Vergil's works after his death. Quintilius Varus had, like Varius, come from Cremona, known Catullus intimately, and, if we accept the view of Servius for the sixth *Eclogue,* had been Vergil's most devoted companion in Siro's school. He also took some part in the civil wars, and came to be looked upon as a very firm supporter of sound literary standards.[1] Horace's *Quis desiderio,* shows that Varus was one of Vergil's most devoted friends.

[1] Cf. Horace, *Ars Poetica,* 440.

Vergil's position as foremost of these poets was doubtless established by the publication of the *Eclogues*. They took Rome by storm, and were even set to music and sung on the stage, according to an Alexandrian fashion then prevailing in the capital. Octavian was, of course, attracted to them by a personal interest. The poet was given a house in Maecenas' gardens on the Esquiline with the hope of enticing him to Rome. Vergil doubtless spent some time in the city before he turned to the more serious task of the *Georgics*, but we are told that he preferred the Neapolitan bay and established his home there. This group, it would seem, was definitely drawn into Octavian's circle soon after the peace of Brundisium, and formed the nucleus of a kind of literary academy that set the standards for the Augustan age.

The introduction of Horace into this circle makes an interesting story. He was five years younger than Vergil, and had had his advanced education at Athens. There Brutus found him in 43, when attending philosophical lectures in order to hide his political intrigues; and though Horace was a freedman's son, Brutus gave him the high dignity of a military tribuneship. Brutus as a Republican was, of course, a stickler for all the aristocratic customs. That he conferred upon Horace a knight's office probably indicates that the *libertinus pater* had been a war captive rather than a man of servile stock, and, therefore, only technically a " freedman." In practical life the Romans observed this distinction, even though it was not usually feasible to do so in political life. After Philippi Horace found himself with the defeated remnant and returned to Italy only to discover that his property had been confiscated. He was eager for a career in literature, but having to earn his bread, he bought a poor clerkship in the treasury office. Then during spare moments he wrote — satires, of course. What else could such a wreckage of enthusiasm and ambitions produce?

His only hope lay in attracting the attention of some kindly disposed literary man, and for some reason he chose Vergil. The *Eclogues* were not yet out, but the *Culex* was in circulation, and he made the pastoral scene of this the basis of an epode — the second — written with no little good-natured humor. Horace imagines a broker of the forum reading that passage, and, quite carried away by the succession of delightful scenes, deciding to quit business for the simple life. He accordingly draws in all his moneys on the Calends — on the Ides he lends them out again! [2] What Vergil wrote Horace

[2] Horace's scenes (his memory is visual rather than auditory) unmistakably reproduce those of the *Culex*; cf. *Culex* 148-58 with *Epode* 26-28; *Culex* 86-7 with *Epode* 21-22; *Culex*

when he received a copy of the *Epode*, we are not told, but in his next work, the *Georgics*, he returned the compliment by similarly threading Horace's phrases into a description of country life — a passage that is indeed one of the most successful in the book.[3]

The composition of the sixteenth epode by Horace — soon after the second, it would seem — gave Vergil an opportunity to recognize the new poet, and answer his pessimistic appeal with the cheerful prophecy of the fourth *Eclogue*, as we have seen. By this time we may suppose that an intimate friendship had sprung up between the two poets, strengthened of course by friendly intercourse, now that Vergil could spend some of his time at Rome. Horace himself tells how Vergil and Varius introduced him to Maecenas (*Sat.* I. 6), an important event in his career that took place some time before the Brundisian journey (*Sat.* I. 5). Maecenas had hesitated somewhat before accepting the intimacy of the young satirist: Horace had fought quite recently in the enemy's army, had criticized the government in his *Epodes*, and was of

---

49–50 with *Epode* 11–12; etc. A full comparison is made in *Classical Philology*, 1920, p. 24. Vergil could, of course, be expected to recognize the allusions to his own poem.

[3] See *Georgics*, II, 458–542, and a discussion of it in *Classical Philology*, 1920, p. 42.

a class — at least technically — which Octavian had been warned not to recognize socially, unless he was prepared to offend the old nobility. But Horace's dignified candor won him the confidence of Maecenas; and that there might be no misunderstanding he included in his first book of *Satires* a simple account of what he was and hoped to be. Thus through the efforts of Vergil and Varius he entered the circle whose guiding spirit he was destined to become.

Thus the coterie was formed, which under such powerful patronage was bound to become a sort of unofficial commission for the regulation of literary standards. It was an important question, not only for the young men themselves but for the future of Roman literature, which direction this group would take and whose influence would predominate. It might be Maecenas, the holder of the purse-strings, a man who could not check his ambition to express himself whether in prose or verse. This Etruscan, whose few surviving pages reveal the fact that he never acquired an understanding of the dignity of Rome's language, that he was temperamentally un-Roman in his love for meretricious gaudiness and prettiness, might have worked incalculable harm on this school had his taste in the least affected it. But whether he withheld his dictum, or it was disre-

garded by the others, no influence of his can be de-
tected in the literature of the epoch.

Apollodorus, Octavian's aged teacher, a man of
very great personal influence, and highly respected,
probably counted for more. In his lectures and his
books, one of which, Valgius, a member of the circle,
translated into Latin, he preached the doctrines of
a chaste and dignified classicism. His creed fortunately fell in with the tendencies of the time, and
whether this teaching be called a cause, or whether
the popularity of it be an effect of pre-existing
causes, we know that this man came to represent
many of the ideals of the school.

But to trace these ideals in their contact with Vergil's mental development, we must look back for a
moment to the tendencies of the Catullan age from
which he was emerging. In a curious passage written
not many years after this, Horace, when grouping
the poets according to their styles and departments,[4]
places Vergil in a class apart. He mentions first a
turgid epic poet for whom he has no regard. Then
there are Varius and Pollio, in epic and tragedy
respectively, of whose forceful directness he does
approve. In comedy, his friend, Fundanius, represents a homely plainness which he commends, while
Vergil stands for gentleness and urbanity (molle
atque facetum).

[4] *Sat.* I. 10, 40 ff.

The passage is important not only because it reveals a contemporaneous view of Vergil's position but because it shows Horace thus early as the spokesman of the " classical " coterie, the tenets of which in the end prevailed. In this passage Horace employs the categories of the standard text-books of rhetoric of that day [5] which were accustomed to classify styles into four types: (1) Grand and ornate, (2) grand but austere, (3) plain and austere, (4) plain but graceful. The first two styles might obviously be used in forensic prose or in ambitious poetic work like epics and tragedies. Horace would clearly reject the former, represented for instance by Hortensius and Pacuvius, in favor of the austere dignity and force of the second, affected by men like Cornificius in prose and Varius and Pollio in verse. The two types of the " plain " style were employed in more modest poems of literature, both in prose and in such poetry as comedy, the epyllion, in pastoral verse, and the like. Severe simplicity was favored by Calvus in his orations, Catullus in his lyrics; while a more polished and well-nigh *précieuse* plainness was illustrated in the speeches of Calidius and in the Alexandrian epyllion of Catullus' *Peleus and Thetis* and in Vergil's *Ciris* and *Bucolics*.

[5] E. g. Demetrius, Philodemus, Cicero; cf. *Class. Phil.* 1920, p. 230.

In choosing between these two, Horace, of course, sympathizes with the ideals of the severe and chaste style, which he finds in the comedies of Fundanius. Vergil's early work, unambitious and "plain" though it is, falls, of course, into the last group; and though Horace recognizes his type with a friendly remark, one feels that he recognizes it for reasons of friendship, rather than because of any native sympathy for it. By his juxtaposition he shows that the classical ideals of the second and third of the four "styles" are to him most sympathetic. *Mollitudo* does not find favor in any of his own work, or in his criticism of other men's work. Vergil, therefore, though he appears in this Augustan coterie as an important member, is still felt to be something of a free lance who adheres to Alexandrian art [6] not wholly in accord with the standards which are now being formulated. If Horace had obeyed his literary instincts alone he would probably have relegated Vergil at this period to the silence he accorded Gallus and Propertius if not to the open hostility he expressed towards the Alexandrianism of Catullus. It is significant of Vergil's breadth of sympathy that he remitted not a jot in his devotion to Catullus and Gallus and that he won the deep

[6] Horace had doubtless seen not only the *Culex* but several of the other minor works that Vergil never deigned to put into general circulation.

reverence of Propertius while remaining the friend
and companion of the courtly group working towards a stricter classicism. If we may attempt to
classify the early Augustans, we find them align-
ing themselves thus. The strict classicists are Horace the satirist, Varius a writer of epics, Pollio of
tragedy; while Varus, Valgius, Plotius, and Fundanius, though less productive, employ their influence in the support of this tendency as does Tibullus
somewhat later. Vergil is a close personal friend
of these men but refuses to accept the axioms of any
one school; Gallus, his friend, is a free romanticist,
and is followed in this tendency a few years later
by Propertius.

The influences that made for classicism were
many. Apollodorus, the teacher of Octavian, must
have been a strong factor, but since his work has
been lost, the weight of it cannot now be estimated.
Horace imbibed his love for severe ideals in Athens,
of course. There his teachers were Stoic rhetoricians who trained him in an uncompromising respect
for stylistic rules.[7] He read the Hellenistic poets,
to be sure, and reveals in his poems a ready memory of them, but it was the great epoch of Greek

[7] For the stylistic tenets of the Stoic teachers see Fiske,
Lucilius and Horace, pp. 64-143. Apollodorus seems to be the
rhetorician whom Horace calls Heliodorus in *Sat.* I, 5, see
Class. Phil. 1920, 393.

poetry that formed his style.   Such are the foreign
influences.   But the native Roman factors must not
be forgotten.   In point of fact it was the classicistic
Catullus and Calvus, of the simple, limpid lyrics,
written in pure unalloyed every-day Latin, that
taught the new generation to reject the later Hellenistic style of Catullus and Calvus as illustrated
in the verse romances.   Varus, Pollio, and Varius
were old enough to know Catullus and Calvus per-
sonally, to remember the days when poems like
Dianae sumus in fide were just issued, and they
were poets who could value the perfect art of such
work even after the authors of them had been enticed by ambition into dangerous by-paths.   In a
word, it was Catullus and Calvus, the lyric poets,
who made it possible for the next generation to reject Catullus and Calvus the neoteric romancers.

For the modern, therefore, it is difficult to restrain a just resentment when he finds Horace re-
ferring to these two great predecessors with a sneer.
Yet we can, if we will, detect an adequate
explanation of Horace's attitude.   Very few poets
of any time have been able to capture and hold the
generation immediately succeeding.   The stronger
the impression made by a genius, the farther away
is the pendulum of approbation apt to swing.   The
neoteroi had to face, in addition to this revulsion,

the misfortunes of the time. The civil wars which
came close upon them had little use for the sentimentality of their romances or the involutions of
their manner of composition. And again, Catullus
and Calvus had been over-brutal in their attacks
upon Julius Caesar, a character lifted to the high
heavens by the war and the martyrdom that followed. And, as fortune would have it, almost all
of the new literary men were, as we have seen, pe-
culiarly devoted to Caesar. We know enough of
wars to have discovered that intense partizanship
does silence literary judgment except in the case
of a very few men of unusual balance. Vergil was
one of the very few; he kept his candle lit at the
shrine of Catullus still, but this was hardly to be
expected of the rest.

In prose also the Augustans upheld the refined
and chaste work of classical Atticism, an ideal which
they derived from the Romans of the preceding
generation rather than from teachers like Apollodorus. Pollio and Messalla are now the foremost
orators. Pollio had stood close to Calvus as well
as to Caesar, and had witnessed the revulsion of
feeling against Cicero's style which continued to
move in its old leisurely course even after the civil
war had quickened men's pulses. Messalla may
have been influenced by the example of his general,

Brutus, a man who never wasted words (so long as he kept his temper). Messalla and Pollio were the dictators of prose style during this period.

We find Vergil, therefore, in a peculiar position. He was still recognized as a pupil of Catullus and the Alexandrians at a time when the pendulum was swinging so violently away from the republican poets that they did not even get credit for the lessons that they had so well taught the new generation. Vergil himself was in each new work drifting more and more toward classicism, but he continued to the last to honor Catullus and Calvus, Cinna and Cornificius, and his friend Gallus, in complimentary imitation or by friendly mention. The new Academy was proud to claim him as a member, though it doubtless knew that Vergil was too great to be bound by rules. To after ages, while Horace has come to stand as an extremist who carried the law beyond the spirit, Vergil, honoring the past and welcoming the future, has assumed the position of Rome's most representative poet.

XIV

THE "GEORGICS"

THE years that followed the publication of the *Eclogues* seem to have been a season of reading, traveling, observing, and brooding. Maecenas desired to keep the poet at Rome, and as an inducement provided him with a villa in his own gardens on the Esquiline. The fame of the *digitus praetereuntium* awaited his coming and going, his *Bucolics* had been set to music and sung in the concert halls to vehement applause.[1] He seems even to have made an effort to be socially congenial. There is intimate knowledge of courtly customs in the staging of his epic; and in Horace's fourth book a refurbished early poem in Philodemus' manner pictures a Vergil — apparently the poet — as the pet of the fashionable world. But these things had no attraction for him. Rome indeed appealed to his imagination, *Roma pulcherrima rerum*, but it

---

[1] Tacitus, *Dialogus*, 13: Malo securum et quietum Vergilii secessum, in quo tamen neque apud divum Augustum gratia caruit neque apud populum Romanum notitia. Testes Augusti epistulae, testis ipse populus, qui auditis in theatro Vergilii versibus surrexit universus et forte praesentem spectantemque Vergilium veneratus est quasi Augustum.

was the invisible Rome rather than the *fumum et opes strepitumque,* it was the city of pristine ideals, of irresistible potency, of Anchises' pageant of heroes. When he walked through the Forum he saw not only the glistening monuments in their new marble veneer, but beyond these, in the far distant past, the straw hut of Romulus and the sacred grove on the Capitoline where the spirit of Jove had guarded a folk of simpler piety.[2] And down the centuries he beheld the heroes, the law-givers, and the rulers, who had made the Forum the court of a world-wide empire. The Rome of his own day was too feverish, it soon drove him back to his garden villa near Naples.

It was well that he possessed such a retreat during those years of petty political squabbles. The capital still hummed with rumors of civil war. Antony seemed determined to sever the eastern provinces from the empire and make of them a gift to Cleopatra and her children — a mad course that could only end in another world war. Sextus Pompey still held Sicily and the central seas, ready to betray the state at the first mis-step on Octavian's part. At Rome itself were many citizens in high position who were at variance with the government, quite prepared to declare for Antony or Pompey

[2] *Aeneid* VIII.

if either should appear a match for the young heir
of Caesar. Clearly the great epic of Rome could
not have matured in that atmosphere of suspicion,
intrigue, and selfishness. The convulsions of the
dying republic, beheld day by day near at hand,
could only have inspired a disgust sufficient to poison
a poet's sensitive hope. It was indeed fortunate
that Vergil could escape all this, that he could re-
tain through the period of transition the memories
of Rome's former greatness and the faith in her
destiny that he had imbibed in his youth. The
time came when Octavian, after Actium, reunited
the Empire with a firm hand and justified the buoyant optimism which Vergil, almost alone of his generation, had been able to preserve.

During these few years Vergil seems to have
written but little. We have, however, a strange
poem of thirty-eight lines, the *Copa*, which, to
judge from its exclusion from the *Catalepton*,
should perhaps be assigned to this period. A study
in tempered realism, not unlike the eighth *Eclogue*,
it gives us the song of a Syrian tavern-maid inviting
wayfarers into her inn from the hot and dusty road.
The spirit is admirably reproduced in Kirby Smith's
rollicking translation:[3]

[3] See Kirby Flower Smith, *Martial, the Epigrammatist and
Other Essays*, Johns Hopkins Press, 1920, p. 170. The attribution of the poem to Vergil by the ancients as well as by

'Twas at a smoke-stained tavern, and she, the hostess
    there —
A wine-flushed Syrian damsel, a turban on her hair —
Beat out a husky tempo from reeds in either hand,
And danced — the dainty wanton — an Ionian saraband.
" 'Tis hot," she sang, " and dusty; nay, travelers, whither
    bound?
Bide here and tip a beaker — till all the world goes round;
Bide here and have for asking wine-pitchers, music, flowers,
Green pergolas, fair gardens, cool coverts, leafy bowers.
In our Arcadian grotto we have someone to play
On Pan-pipes, shepherd fashion, sweet music all the day.
We broached a cask but lately; our busy little stream
Will gurgle softly near you the while you drink and
    dream.
Chaplets of yellow violets a-plenty you shall find,
And glorious crimson roses in garlands intertwined;
And baskets heaped with lilies the water nymph shall
    bring —
White lilies that this morning were mirrored in her spring.
Here's cheese new pressed in rushes for everyone who
    comes,
And, lo, Pomona sends us her choicest golden plums.
Red mulberries await you, late purple grapes withal,
Dark melons cased in rushes against the garden wall,
Brown chestnuts, ruddy apples. Divinities bide here,
Fair Ceres, Cupid, Bacchus, those gods of all good cheer,
Priapus too — quite harmless, though terrible to see —
Our little hardwood warden with scythe of trusty tree.

---

the manuscripts, and the style of its fanciful realism so patent
in much of Vergil's work place the poem in the authentic list.
Rand, *Young Virgil's Poetry*, Harvard Studies, 1919, p. 174,
has well summed up the arguments regarding the authorship
of the poem.

Ho, friar with the donkey, turn in and be our guest!
Your donkey — Vesta's darling — is weary; let him rest.
In every tree the locusts their shrilling still renew,
And cool beneath the brambles the lizard lies perdu.
So test our summer-tankards, deep draughts for thirsty
    men;
Then fill our crystal goblets, and souse yourself again.
Come, handsome boy, you're weary! 'Twere best for
    you to twine
Your heavy head with roses and rest beneath our vine,
Where dainty arms expect you and fragrant lips invite;
Oh, hang the strait-laced model that plays the anchorite!
Sweet garlands for cold ashes why should you care to
    save?
Or would you rather keep them to lay upon your grave?
Nay, drink and shake the dice-box. Tomorrow's care
    begone!
Death plucks your sleeve and whispers: ' Live now, I come
    anon.' "

Memories of the Neapolitan bay! The *Copa* should
be read in the arbor of an *osteria* at Sorrento or Ca-
pri to the rhythm of the tarantella where the modern
offspring of Vergil's tavern-maid are still plying
the arts of song and dance upon the passerby.[4]

[4] Unfortunately the evidence does not suffice to assign the
Moretum to Vergil, though it was certainly composed by a
genuine if somewhat halting poet, and in Vergil's day. It
has many imaginative phrases, and the meticulous exactness of
its miniature work might seem to be Vergilian were it not for
the unrelieved plainness of the theme. Even so, it might be
considered an experiment in a new style, if the rather dubious
manuscript evidence were supported by a single ancient citation.
See Rand, *loc. cit.* p. 178.

There are also three brief *Priapea* which should probably be assigned to this period. The third may indeed have been an inscription on a pedestal of the scare-crow god set out to keep off thieving rooks and urchins in the poet's own garden:

This place, my lads, I prosper, I guard the hovel, too,
Thatched, as you see, by willows and reeds and grass that
    grew
In all the marsh about it; hence me, mere stump of oak,
Shaped by the farmer's hatchet, they now as god invoke.
They bring me gifts devoutly, the master and his boy,
Supposing me the giver of the blessings they enjoy.
The kind old man each morning comes here to weed the
    ground,
He clears the shrine of thistles and burrs that grow around.
The lad brings dainty offerings with small but ready hand:
At dawn of spring he crowns me with a lavish daisy-strand,
From summer's earliest harvest, while still the stalk is
    green,
He wreathes my brow with chaplets; he fills me baskets
    clean
With golden pansies, poppies, with apples ripe and gourds,
The first rich blushing clusters of grapes for me he hoards.
And once to my great honor — but let no god be told! —
He brought me to my altar a lambkin from the fold.
So though, my lads, a Scare-Crow and no true god I be,
My master and his vineyard are very dear to me.
Keep off your filching hands, lads, and elsewhere ply your
    theft:
Our neighbor is a miser, his Scare-Crow gets no gifts,
His apples are not guarded — the path is on your left.

The quaint simplicity of the sentiment and the playful surprise at the end quickly disarm any skepticism that would deny these lines to Horace's poet of " tender humor."

During this period the poet seems also to have traveled. Maecenas enjoyed the society of literary men, and we may well suppose that he took Vergil with him in his administrative tours on more than the one occasion which Horace happens to have recorded. The poet certainly knows Italy remarkably well. The meager and inaccurate maps and geographical works of that day could not have provided him with the insight into details which the *Georgics* and the last six books of the *Aeneid* reveal. We know, of course, from Horace's third ode that Vergil went to Greece. This famous poem, a " steamer-letter " as it were, is undated, but it may well be a continuation of the Brundisian diary. The strange turn which the poem takes — its dread of the sea's dangers — seems to point to a time when Horace's memories of his own shipwreck were still very vivid.

There was also time for extensive reading. That Vergil ranged widely and deeply in philosophy and history, antiquities and all the world's best prose and poetry, the vast learning of the *Georgics* and the *Aeneid* abundantly proves. The epic story which he had early plotted out must have lain very near the threshold of his consciousness through this period, for his mind kept seizing upon and storing up apposite incidents and germs of fruitful lore. References to Aeneas crop out here and there in the *Georgics,* and the mysterious address to Mantua in the third book promises, under allusive metaphors, an epic of Trojan heroes. Nor could the poet forget the philosophic work he had so long pondered over. Doubts increased, however, of his capacity to justify himself after the sure success of Lucretius. A remarkable confession in the second book of the *Georgics* reveals his conviction that in this poem he had, through lack of confidence, chosen the inferior theme of nature's physical and sensuous appeal when he would far rather have experienced the intellectual joy of penetrating into nature's inner mysteries.[5]

Though we need not take too literally a poet's prefatorial remarks, Vergil doubtless hoped that his

---

[5] Me vero primum dulces ante omnia Musae,
   Quarum sacra fero ingenti percussus amore,
   Accipiant, caelique vias et sidera monstrent —
   Sin, has ne possim naturae accedere partes,
   Frigidus obstiterit circum praecordia sanguis,
   Rura mihi et rigui placeant in vallibus amnes.
                                    Georgics, II. 475. ff.

Was this striking *apologia* of the *Georgics* forced upon Vergil by the fact that in the *Aetna,* 264-74, he had pronounced peasant-lore trivial in comparison with science?

Georgics might turn men's thoughts towards a serious effort at rehabilitating agriculture, and the practical-minded Maecenas certainly encouraged the work with some such aim in view. The government might well be deeply concerned. The veterans who had recently settled many of Italy's best tracts could not have been skilled farmers. The very fact that the lands were given them for political services could only have suggested to the shrewd among them that the old Roman respect for property rights had been infringed, and that it was wise to sell as soon as possible and depart with some tangible gain before another revolution resulted in a new redistribution. Such suspicions could hardly beget the patience essential for the development of agriculture. And yet this was the very time when farming must be encouraged. Large parts of the arable land had been abandoned to grazing during the preceding century because of the importation of the provincial stipendiary grain, and Italy had lost the custom of raising the amount of food that her population required. As a result, the younger Pompey's control of Sicily and the trade routes had now brought on a series of famines and consequent bread-riots. Year after year Octavian failed in his attempts to lure away or to defeat this obnoxious rebel. At best he could buy him off for a while,

though he never knew at what season of scarcity
the purchase price might become prohibitive. The
choice of Vergil's subject coincided, therefore, with
a need that all men appreciated.

The *Georgics*, however, are not written in the
spirit of a colonial advertisement.   In the youthful
Culex Vergil had dwelt somewhat too emphatically
upon the song-birds and the cool shade, and had
drawn upon himself the genial comment of Horace
that Alfius did not find conditions in the country
quite as enchanting as pictured.   This time the poet
paints no idealized landscape.   Enticing though the
picture is, Vergil insists on the need of unceasing,
ungrudging toil.   He lists the weeds and blights,
the pests and the vermin against which the farmer
must contend.   Indeed it is in the contemplation
of a life of toil that he finds his honest philosophy
of life: the gospel of salvation through work.
Hardships whet the ingenuity of man; God himself
for man's own good brought an end to the age of
golden indolence, shook the honey from the trees,
and gave vipers their venom.   Man has been left
alone to contend with an obstinate nature, and in
that struggle to discover his own worth.   The
Georgics are far removed from pastoral allegory;
Italy is no longer Arcadia, it is just Italy in all its
glory and all its cruelty.

Vergil's delight in nature is essentially Roman, though somewhat more self-conscious than that of his fellows. There is little of the sentimental rapture that the eighteenth century discovered for us. Vergil is not likely to stand in postures before the awful solemnity of the sea or the majesty of wide vistas from mountain tops. Italian hill-tops afford views of numerous charming landscapes but no scenes of entrancing grandeur or awe-inspiring desolation, and the sea, before the days of the compass, was too suggestive of death and sorrow to invite consideration of its lawless beauty. These aspects of nature had to be discovered by later experiences in other lands. At first glance Vergil seems to care most for the obvious gifts of Italy's generous amenities, the physical pleasure in the free out-of-doors, the form and color of landscapes, the wholesome life. As one reads on, however, one becomes aware of an intimacy and fellowship with animate things that go deeper. Particularly in the second book the very blades of grass and tendrils of the vines seem to be sentient. The grafted trees "behold with wonder" strange leaves and fruits growing from their stems, transplanted shoots "put off their wild-wood instincts," the thirsting plant "lifts up its head" in gratitude when watered. Our own generation, which was sedulously enticed into nature study by books crammed with the "pathetic fallacy," has become suspicious of everything akin to "nature faking." It has learned that this device has been a trick employed by a crafty pedagogy for the sake of appealing to unimaginative children. Vergil was probably far from being conscious of any such purpose. As a Roman he simply gave expression to a mode of viewing nature that still seemed natural to most Greeks and Romans. The Roman farmer had not entirely outgrown his primitive animism. When he said his prayers to the spirits of the groves, the fields, and the streams, he probably did not visualize these beings in human form; manifestations of life betokened spirits that produced life and growth. Vergil's phrases are the poetic expression of the animism of the unsophisticated rustic which at an earlier age had shaped the great nature myths.

And if Vergil had been questioned about his own faith he could well have found a consistent answer. Though he had himself long ceased to pay homage to these *animae*, his philosophy, like that of Lucretius, also sought the life-principle in nature, though he sought that principle a step farther removed in the atom, the vitalized seeds of things, forever in motion, forever creating new combinations, and forever working the miracles of life by means of the energy with which they were themselves instinct. The memorable lines on spring in the second book are cast into the form of old poetry, but the basis of them is Epicurean energism, as in Lucretius' prooemium. Vergil's study of evolution had for him also united man and nature, making the romance of the *Georgics* possible; it had shaped a kind of scientific animism that permitted him to accept the language of the simple peasant even though its connotations were for him more complex and subtle.

Finally, the careful reader will discover in Vergil's nature poetry a very modern attention to details such as we hardly expect to find before the nineteenth century. Here again Vergil is Lucretius' companion. This habit was apparently a composite product. The ingredients are the capacity for wonder that we find in some great poets like Wordsworth and Plato, a genius for noting details, bred in him as in Lucretius by long occupation with deductive methods of philosophy, — scientific pursuits have thus enriched modern poetry also — and a sure aesthetic sense. This power of observation has been overlooked by many of Vergil's commentators. Conington, for example, has frequently done the poet an injustice by assuming that Vergil was in error whenever his statements seem not to accord with what we happen to know. We have

now learned to be more wary. It is usually a safer
assumption that our observation is in error. A recent study of " trees, shrubs and plants of Vergil,"
illuminating in numberless details, has fallen into
the same error here and there by failing to notice
that Vergil wrote his *Bucolics* and *Georgics* not near
Mantua but in southern Italy. The modern botan-
ical critic of Vergil should, as Mackail has said,
study the flora of Campania not of Lombardy. In
every line of composition Vergil took infinite pains
to give an accurate setting and atmosphere. Carcopino [6] has just astonished us with proof of the
poet's minute study of topographical details in the
region of Lavinium and Ostia, Mackail [7] has vindi-
cated his care as an antiquarian, Warde Fowler [8]
has repeatedly pointed out his scrupulous accuracy
in portraying religious rites, and now Sergeaunt,[9]
in a study of his botany, has emphasized his habit
of making careful observations in that domain.

This modern habit it is that makes the *Georgics*
read so much like Fabre's remarkable essays. The
study of the bees in the fourth book is, of course,
not free from errors that nothing less than genera-

[6] Carcopino, *Virgile et les origines d'Ostie.*
[7] Mackail, *Journal of Roman Studies,* 1915.
[8] Warde Fowler, *Religious Experience of the Roman People,*
p. 408.
[9] Sergeaunt, *Trees, Shrubs, and Plants of Virgil.*

tions of close scrutiny could remove. But the right kind of observing has begun. On the other hand the book is not merely a farmer's practical manual on how to raise bees for profit. The poet's interest is in the amazing insects themselves, their how and why and wherefore. It is the mystery of their instincts, habits, and all-compelling energy that leads him to study the bees, and finally to the half-concealed confession that his philosophy has failed to solve the problems of animate nature.

XV

THE AENEID

W<small>HILE</small> Caesar Octavian, now grown to full political stature, was reuniting the East and the West after Actium, Vergil was writing the last pages of the *Georgics*. The battle that decided Rome's future also determined the poet's next theme. The Epic of Rome, abandoned at the death of Caesar, unthinkable during the civil wars which followed, appealed for a hearing now that Rome was saved and the empire restored. Vergil's youthful enthusiasm for Rome, which had sprung from a critical reading of her past career, seemed fully justified; he began at once his *Arma virumque*.

The *Aeneid* reveals, as the critics of nineteen centuries have reiterated, an unsurpassed range of reading. But it is not necessary to repeat the evidence of Vergil's literary obligations in an essay concerned chiefly with the poet's more intimate experiences. In point of fact, the tracking of poetic reminiscences in a poet who lived when no concealment of borrowed thought was demanded does as much violence to Vergil as it does to Euripides or Petrarch. The poet has always been expected to give expression to his own convictions, but until recently it has been considered a graceful act on his part to honor the good work of his predecessors by the frank use, in recognizable form, of the lines that he most admires. The only requirement has been that the poet should assimilate, and not merely agglomerate his acceptances, that he should as Vergil put it, " wrest the club from Hercules " and wield it as its master.

In essence the poetry of the *Aeneid* is never Homeric, despite the incorporation of many Homeric lines. It is rather a sapling of Vergil's Hellenistic garden, slowly acclimated to the Italian soil, fed richly by years of philosophic study, braced, pruned, and reared into a tree of noble strength and classic dignity. The form and majesty of the tree bespeak infinite care in cultivation, but the fruit has not lost the delicate tang and savour of its seed. The poet of the *Ciris*, the *Copa*, the *Dirae*, and the *Bucolics* is never far to seek in the *Aeneid*.

It would be a long story to trace the flowering in the *Aeneid* of the seedling sown in Vergil's boyhood garden-plot.[1] The note of intimacy, unexpected in an epic, the occasional drawing of the veil

[1] For a careful study of this subject see Duckett, *Hellenistic Influence on the Aeneid*, Smith College Studies, 1920.

to reveal the poet's own countenance, an un-Homeric
sentimentality now and then, the great abundance
of sense-teeming collocations, the depth of sympathy
revealed in such tragic characters as Pallas, Lausus,
Euryalus, the insistent study of inner motives, the
meticulous selection of incidents, the careful artistry
of the meter, the fastidious choice of words, and
the precision of the joiner's craft in the composition
of traditional elements, all suggest the habits of
work practiced by the friends of Cinna and Valerius
Cato.

The last point is well illustrated in Sinon's speech
at the opening of the second book.   The old folk-
tale of how the " wooden horse," left on the shore
by the Greeks, was recklessly dragged to the citadel
by the Trojans satisfied the unquestioning Homer.
Vergil does not take the improbable on faith. Sinon
is compelled to be entirely convincing. In his
speech he uses every art of persuasion: he awakens
in turn curiosity, surprise, pity, admiration, sympathy, and faith.   The passage is as curiously
wrought as any episode of Catullus or the *Ciris*.   It
is not, as has been held, a result of rhetorical studies
alone; it reveals rather a native good sense tempered
with a neoteric interest in psychology and a neoteric
exactness in formal composition.   And yet the passage exhibits a great advance upon the geometric

formality of the *Ciris*. The incident is not treated episodically as it might have been in Vergil's early work. The pattern is not whimsically intricate but is shaped by an understanding mind. While its art is as studied and conscious as that of the *Ciris*, it has the directness and integrity of Homeric narrative. Yet Vergil has not forgotten the startling effects that Catullus would attain by compressing a long tale into a suggestive phrase, if only a memory of the tale could be assumed. The story of Priam's death on the citadel is told in all its tragic horror till the climax is reached. Then suddenly with astonishing force the mind is flung through and beyond the memories of the awful mutilation by the amazingly condensed phrase:

Jacet ingens litore truncus
avulsumque umeris caput et sine nomine corpus.

There Vergil has given only the last line of a suppressed tragedy which the reader is compelled to visualize for himself.

Neoteric, too, is the accurate observation and the patience with details displayed by the author of the *Aeneid*. In his youth Vergil had, to be sure, avoided the extremes of photographic realism illustrated by the very curious *Moretum*, but he had nevertheless, in works like the *Copa*, the *Dirae*, and

the eighth *Eclogue,* practiced the craft of the mini-
aturist whenever he found the minutiae aesthetically
significant.   To realize the precision of his strokes
even then one has but to recall the couplet of the
Copa which in an instant sets one upon the dusty
road of an Italian July midday:

> Nunc cantu crebro rumpunt arbusta cicadae
> nunc varia in gelida sede lacerta latet.

Throughout the *Aeneid,* the patches of landscape, the retreats for storm-tossed ships, the carved
temple-doors, the groups of accoutred warriors
marching past, and many a gruesome battle scene,
are reminders of this early technique.

What degrees of conscientious workmanship went
into these results, we are just now learning.   Carcopino,[2] who, with a copy of Vergil in hand, has
carefully surveyed the Latin coast from the Tiber
mouth, past the site of Lavinium down to Ardea, is
convinced that the poet traced every manoeuvre and
every sally on the actual ground which he chose for
his theatre of action in the last six books.   It still
seems possible to recognize the deep valley of the
ambuscade and the plain where Camilla deployed
her cavalry.   Furthermore, there can be little doubt
that for the sake of a heroic-age setting Vergil

[2] Carcopino, *Virgile et les origines d'Ostie.*

studied the remains and records of most ancient Rome. There were still in existence in various Latin towns sixth-century temples laden with antique arms and armor deposited as votive offerings, terracotta statues of gods and heroes, and even documents stored for safe-keeping. In the expansion of Rome over the Campus Martius unmarked tombs with their antique furniture were often disclosed. It is apparent from his works that Vergil examined such material, just as he delved into Varro's antiquities and Cato's " origins " for ancient lore. His remarks on Praeneste and Antemnae, his knowledge of ancient coin symbols, of the early rites of the Hercules cult, show the results of these early habits of work. It must always be noticed, however, that in his mature art he is master of his vast hoard of material. There is never, as in the *Culex* and *Ciris*, a display of irrelevant facts, a yielding to the temptation of being excursive and episodic. Wherever the work had received the final touch, the composition shows a flawless unity.

The poet's response to personal experience reveals itself nowhere more than in the political aspect of the *Aeneid*, a fact that is the more remarkable because Vergil lived so long in Epicurean circles where an interest in politics was studiously suppressed.

What makes the poem the first of national epics is, however, not a devotion to Rome's historical claims to primacy in Italy. The narrow imperialism of the urban aristocracy finds no support in him. Not the city of Rome but Italy is the *patria* of the *Aeneid*, and Italy as a civilizing and peace-bringing force, not as the exploiting conqueror. Here we recognize a spirit akin to Julius Caesar. Vergil's hero Aeneas, is not a Latin but a Trojan. That fact is, of course, due to the exigencies of tradition, but that Aeneas receives his aid from the Greek Evander and from the numerous Etruscan cities north of the Tiber while most of the Latins join Turnus, the enemy, cannot be attributed to tradition. In fact, Livy, who gives the more usual Roman version, says nothing of the Greeks, but joins Latinus and the Latian aborigines to Aeneas while he musters the Etruscans under the Rutulian, Turnus. The explanation for Vergil's striking departure from the usual patriotic version of the legend is rather involved and need not be examined here. But we may at any rate remark his wish to recognize the many races that had been amalgamated by the state, to refuse his approval of a narrow urban patriotism, and to give his assent to a view of Rome's place and mission upon which Julius Caesar had always acted in extending citizenship to peoples of all races, in scattering Roman colonies throughout the empire, and in setting the provinces on the road to a full participation in imperial privileges and duties. With such a policy Vergil, schooled at Cremona, Milan, and Naples, could hardly fail to sympathize.

It has been inferred from the position of authority which Aeneas assumes that Vergil favored a strong monarchial form of government and intended Aeneas to be, as it were, a prototype of Augustus. The inference is doubtless over-hasty. Vergil had a lively historical sense and in his hero seems only to have attempted a picture of a primitive king of the heroic age. Indeed Aeneas is perhaps more of an autocrat than are the Homeric kings, but that is because the Trojans are pictured as a migrating group, torn root and branch from their land and government, and following a semi-divine leader whose directions they have deliberately chosen to obey. In his references to Roman history, in the pageant of heroes of the sixth book, as well as in the historical scenes of the shield, no monarchial tendencies appear. Brutus the tyrannicide, Pompey and Cato, the irreconcilable foes of Caesar, Vergil's youthful hero, receive their meed of praise in the *Aeneid*, though there were many who held it treason in that day to mention rebels with respect.

It is indeed a very striking fact that Vergil, who

was the first of Roman writers to attribute divine
honors to the youthful Octavian, refrains entirely
from doing so in the *Aeneid*, at a time when the rest
of Rome hesitated at no form of laudation. Julius
Caesar is still recognized as more than human,

> vocabitur hic quoque votis,

but Augustus is not. The contrast is significant.
The language of the very young man at Naples had,
of course, been colored by Oriental forms of expression that were in part unconsciously imbibed from
the conversations of the Garden. These were
phrases too which Julius Caesar in the last two years
of his life encouraged; for he had learned from
Alexander's experience that the shortest cut through
constitutional obstructions to supreme power lay by
way of the doctrine of divine royalty. In fact, the
Senate was forced to recognize the doctrine before
Caesar's death, and after his death consistently voted
public sacrifices at his grave. Vergil was, therefore,
following a high authority in the case of Caesar, and
was drawing the logical inference in the case of
Octavian when he wrote the first *Eclogue* and the
prooemium of the *Georgics*. This makes it all the
more remarkable that while his admiration for
Augustus increased with the years, he ceased to give
any countenance to the growing cult of " emperor

worship." That the restraint was not simply in obedience to a governmental policy seems clear, for Horace, who in his youthful work had shown his distrust of the government, had now learned to make very liberal use of celestial appellatives.

Augustus, then, is not in any way identified with the semi-divine Aeneas. Vergil does not even place him at a post of special honor on the mount of revelations, but rather in the midst of a long line of remarkable *principes*. With dignity and sanity he lays the stress upon the great events of the Republic and upon its heroes. We may, therefore, justly conclude that when he wrote the epic he advocated a constitution of the type proposed by Cicero, in which the *princeps* should be a true leader in the state but in a constitutional republic.

It is the great past, illustrated by the pageant of heroes and the prophetic pictures of Aeneas's shield, that kindles the poet's imagination. His sympathies are generous enough to include every race within the empire and every leader who had shared in Rome's making, from the divine founder, Romulus, and the tyrannicide, Brutus, to the republican martyrs, Cato and Pompey, as well as the restorers of peace, Caesar and Augustus. He has no false patriotism that blinds him to Rome's shortcomings. He frankly admits with regret her failures in arts and

sciences with a modesty that permits of no reference to his own saving work.   What Rome has
done and can do supremely well he also knows: she
can rule with justice, banish violence with law, and
displace war by peace.   After the years of civil wars
which he had lived through in agony of spirit, it is
not strange that such a mission seemed to him supreme.   And that is why the last words of Anchises
to Aeneas are:

> Hae tibi erunt artes: pacisque imponere morem
> Parcere subjectis et debellare superbos.

The tragedy of Dido reveals better perhaps than
any other portion of the *Aeneid* how sensitively the
poet reflected Rome's life and thought rather than
those of his Greek literary sources.   And yet the
irrepressible Servius was so reckless as to say that
the whole book had been " transferred " from Apollonius.   Fortunately we have in this case the alleged
source, and can meet the scholiast with a sweeping
denial.   Both authors portray the love of a woman,
and there the similarity ends.   Apollonius is wholly
dependent upon a literal Cupid and his shafts.
Vergil, to be sure, is so far obedient to Greek con-
vention as to play with the motive — Cupid came to
the banquet in the form of Ascanius — but only
after it was really no longer needed.   The psychol-

ogy of passion's progress in the first book is convincingly expressed for the first time in any literature. Aeneas first receives a full account of Dido's deeds of courage and presently beholds her as she sits upon her throne, directing the work of city building, judging and ruling as lawgiver and administrator, and finally proclaiming mercy for his shipwrecked companions. For her part she, we discover as he does, had long known his story, and in her admiration for his people had chosen the deeds of Trojan heroes for representation upon the temple doors: Sunt lacrimae rerum. The poet simply and naturally leads hero and heroine through the experience of admiration, generous sympathy, and gratitude to an inevitable affection, which at the night's banquet, through a soul-stirring tale told with dignity and heard in rapture, could only ripen into a very human passion.

The vital difference between Vergil's treatment of the theme and Apollonius' may be traced to the difference between the Roman and the Greek family. Into Italy as into Greece had come, many centuries before, hordes of Indo-European migrants from the Danubian region who had carried into the South the wholesome family customs of the North, the very customs indeed out of which the transalpine literature of medieval chivalry later blossomed.

In Greece those social customs — still recognizable in Homer and the early mythology — had in the sixth century been overwhelmed by a back-flow of Aegean society, when the northern aristocracy was compelled to surrender to the native element which constituted the backbone of the democracy. With the re-emergence of the Aegean society, in which woman was relegated to a menial position, the possibility of a genuine romantic literature naturally came to an end.

At Rome there was no such cataclysm during the centuries of the Republic. Here the old stock though somewhat mixed with Etruscans, survived. The ancient aristocracy retained its dominant position in the state and society, and its mores even penetrated downward. They were not stifled by new southern customs welling up from below, at least not until the plebeian element won the support of the founders of the empire, and finally overwhelmed the nobility. At Rome during the Republic there was no question of social inequality between the sexes, for though in law the patriarchal clan-system, imposed by the exigencies of a migrating group, made the father of the family responsible for civil order, no inferences were drawn to the detriment of the mother's position in the household. Nepos once aptly remarked: " Many things are

considered entirely proper here which the Greeks
hold to be indelicate. No Roman ever hesitates to
take his wife with him to a social dinner. In fact,
our women invariably have the seat of honor at
temples and large gatherings. In such matters we
differ wholly from the Greeks."

Indeed the very persistence of a nobility was in
itself a favorable factor in establishing a better position for women. Not only did the accumulation
of wealth in the household and the persistence of
courtly manners demand respect for the *domina* of
the villa, but the transference of noble blood and
of a goodly inheritance of name and land through
the mother's hand were matters of vital importance.
The nobility of the senate moreover long controlled
the foreign policy of the empire, and as the empire
grew the men were called away to foreign parts on
missions and legations. At such times, the lady in
an important household was mistress of large affairs.
It has been pointed out as a significant fact that the
father of the Gracchi was engaged for long years
in ambassadorial and military duties. The training
of the lads consequently fell to the share of Cor-
nelia, a fact which may in some measure account for
the humanitarian interests of those two brilliant re-
formers. The responsibilities that fell upon the
shoulders of such women must have stimulated their

keenest powers and thus won for them the high esteem which, in this case, we know the sons accorded
their mother. One does not soon forget the scene
(Cicero, *Ad Att*. XV, 11) at which Brutus and Cassius together with their wives, Porcia and Tertia,
and Servilia, the mother of Brutus, discussed
momentous decisions with Cicero. When Brutus
stood wavering, Cicero avoiding the issue, and Cassius as usual losing his temper, it was Servilia who
offered the only feasible solution, and it was her
program which they adopted. Is it surprising that
Greek historians like Plutarch could never quite
comprehend the part in Roman politics played by
women like Clodia, Porcia and Terentia? In sheer
despair he usually resorts to the hypotheses of some
personal intrigue for an explanation of their powerful influence.

It is in truth very likely that had Roman literature been permitted to run its own natural course,
without being overwhelmed, as was the Italian literature of the renaissance, it would have progressed
much farther on the road to Romanticism. Apollonius was far more a restraining influence in this
respect than an inspiration. As it is, Vergil's first
and fourth books are as unthinkable in Greek dress
as is the sixth. They constitute a very conspicuous
landmark in the history of literature.

Vergil does not wholly escape the powerful con-
ventions of his Greek predecessors: in his fourth
book, for instance, there are suggestions of the
melodramatic " maiden's lament " so dear to the
music hall gallery of Alexandria. But Vergil,
apparently to his own surprise, permits his Roman
understanding of life to prevail, and transcends his
first intentions as soon as he has felt the grip of the
character he is portraying. Dido quickly emerges
from the rôle of a temptress designed as a last
snare to trap the hero, and becomes a woman who
reveals human laws paramount even to divine
ordinance. Once realizing this the poet sacrifices
even his hero and wrecks his original plot to be true
to his insight into human nature. The confession
of Aeneas, as he departs, that in heeding heaven's
command he has blasphemed against love — *polluto
amore* — how strange a thought for the *pius Aeneas!*
That sentiment was not Greek, it was a new flash of
intuition of the very quality of purest Romance.

The *Aeneid* is also a remarkably religious poem
to have come from one who had devoted so many
enthusiastic years to a materialistic philosophy.
Indeed it is usual to assume that the poet had abandoned his philosophy and turned to Stoicism before
his death. But there is after all no legitimate

ground for this supposition. The *Aeneid* has, of course, none of the scientific fanaticism that mars the *Aetna*, and the poet has grown mellow and tolerant with years, but that he was still convinced of the general soundness of the Epicurean hypotheses seems certain. Many puzzles of the *Aeneid* are at least best explained by that view. The repetition of his creed in the first *Aeneid* ought to warn us that his enthusiasm for the study of *Rerum natura* did not die. Indeed the *Aeneid* is full of Epicurean phrases and notions. The atoms of fire are struck out of the flint (VI, 6), the atoms of light are emitted from the sun (VII, 527, and VIII, 23), early men were born *duro robore* and lived like those described in the fifth book of Lucretius (VIII, 320), and Conington finds almost two hundred reminiscences of Lucretius in the *Aeneid*, the proportion increasing rather than decreasing in the later books.[3]

It is, however, in the interpretation of the word *fatum* and the rôle played by the gods [4] that the test of Vergil's philosophy is usually applied. The

[3] Servius, VI, 264, makes the explicit statement: ex majore parte, Sironem, id est, magistrum Epicureum sequitur.

[4] The passages have been analyzed and discussed frequently. See especially Heinze, *Vergils Epische Technik*, 290 ff., who interprets Zeus as fate; Matthaei, *Class. Quart.* 1917, pp. 11–26, who denies the identity; Drachmann, *Guderne hos Vergil*, 1887; MacInnis, *Class. Rev.* 1910, p. 160, and Warde Fowler, *Aeneas at the Site of Rome*, pp. 122 ff. For a fuller statement of this question see *Am. Jour. Phil.* 1920.

modern equivalent of *fatum* is, as Guyau[5] has said, *determinism*. Determinism was accepted by both schools but with a difference. To the Stoic, *fatum* is a synonym of Providence whose popular name is Zeus. The Epicurean also accepts *fatum* as governing the universe, but it is not teleological, and Zeus is not identified with it but is, like man, subordinated to it. Again, the Stoic is consistently fatalistic. Even man's moral obligations, which are admitted, imply no real freedom in the shaping of results, for though man has the choice between pursuing his end voluntarily (which is virtue) or kicking against the pricks (which is vice), the sum total of his accomplishments is not altered by his choice: *ducunt volentem fata, nolentem trahunt*. On the other hand, Vergil's master, while he affirms the causal nexus for the governance of the universe:

> nec sanctum numen *fati protollere fines*
> posse neque adversus naturae foedera niti

(Lucr. V, 309), posits a spontaneous initiative in the soul-atoms of man:

> quod *fati foedera rumpat*
> ex infinito *ne causam causa sequatur.*

(Lucr. II, 254). If then Vergil were a Stoic his Jupiter should be omnipotent and omniscient and

5 *Morale d'Epicure*, p. 72.

the embodiment of *fatum*, and his human characters must be represented as devoid of independent power; but such ideas are not found in the *Aeneid*.

Jupiter is indeed called " omnipotens " at times, but so are Juno and Apollo, which shows that the term must be used in a relative sense. In a few cases he can grant very great powers as when he tells Venus: Imperium sine fine dedi (I, 278). But very providence he never seems to be. He draws (sortitur) the lots of fate (III, 375), he does not assign them at will, and he unrolls the book of fate and announces what he finds (I, 261). He is powerless to grant Cybele's prayer that the ships may escape decay:

> Cui tanta deo permissa potestas?   (IX, 97.)

He cannot decide the battle between the warriors until he weighs their fates (XII, 725), and in the council of the gods he confesses explicitly his non-interference with the laws of causality:

> Sua cuique exorsa laborem
> Fortunamque ferent. Rex Jupiter omnibus idem.
> Fata viam invenient. (X, 112.)

And here the scholiast naïvely remarks:

> Videtur hic ostendisse aliud esse fata, aliud Jovem.[6]

---

[6] Serv. *ad loc*. MacInnis, *Class. Rev*. 1910, p. 172, cites several other passages to the point in refutation of Heinze.

Again, contrary to the Stoic creed, the poet con-
ceives of his human characters as capable of initiating
action and even of thwarting fate. Aeneas in the
second book rushes into battle on an impulse; he
could forget his fates and remain in Sicily if he
chose (V, 700). He might also remain in Carth-
age, and explains fully why he does not; and Dido,
if left *nescia fati*, might thwart the fates (I, 299),
and finally does, slaying herself before her time [7]
(IV, 696). The Stoic hypothesis seems to break
down completely in such passages.

Can we assume an Epicurean creed with better
success? At least in so far as it places the *foedera
naturae* above the gods and attributes some freedom
of will and action to men, for as we have seen in
both of these matters Vergil agrees with Lucretius.
But there is one apparent difficulty in that Vergil,
contrary to his teacher's usual practice, permits the
interference of the gods in human action. The difficulty is, however, only apparent, if, as Vergil does,
we conceive of these gods simply as heroic and super-
human characters in the drama, accepted from an
heroic age in order to keep the ancient atmosphere
in which Aeneas had lived in men's imagination ever
since Homer first spoke of him. As such characters
they have the power of initiative and the right to

[7] See Matthaei, *Class. Quart.* 1917, p. 19.

interfere in action that Epicurus attributes to men, and in so far as they are of heroic stature their actions may be the more effective. Thus far an Epicurean might well go, and must go in an epic of the heroic age. This is, of course, not the same as saying that Vergil adopted the gods in imitation of Homer or that he needed Olympic machinery because he supposed it a necessary part of the epic technique. Surely Vergil was gifted with as much critical acumen as Lucan. But he had to accept these creatures as subsidiary characters the moment he chose Aeneas as his hero, for Aeneas was the son of Venus who dwelt with the celestials at least a part of the time. Her presence in turn involved Juno and Jupiter and the rest of her daily associates. Furthermore, since the tale was of the heroic age of long ago, the characters must naturally behave as the characters of that day were wont to do, and there were old books like Homer and Hesiod from which every schoolboy had become familiar with their behavior. If the poet wished to make a plausible tale of that period he could no more undertake to modernize his characters than could Tennyson in his *Idylls.* The would-be gods are in the tale not to reveal Vergil's philosophy — they do not — but to orient the reader in the atmosphere in which Aeneas had always been conceived as moving. They perform the same function as the heroic accoutrements and architecture for a correct description of which Vergil visited ancient temples and studied Cato.

Had he chosen a contemporary hero or one less blessed with celestial relatives there is no reason to suppose that he would have employed the super-human personages at all. If this be true it is as uncritical to search for the poet's own conception of divinity in these personages as it would be to infer his taste in furniture from the straw cot which he chooses to give his hero at Evander's hovel. In the epic of primitive Rome the claims of art took precedence over personal creed, and so they would with any true poet; and if any critic were prosaic enough to object, Vergil might have answered with Livy: Datur haec venia antiquitati ut miscendo humana divinis primordia urbium augustiora faciat, and if the inconsistency with his philosophy were stressed he could refer to Lucretius' proemium. It is clear then that while the conceptions of destiny and free-will found in the *Aeneid* are at variance with Stoic creed at every point, they fit readily into the Epicurean scheme of things as soon as we grant what any Epicurean poet would readily have granted that the celestials might be employed as characters of the drama if in general subordinated to the same laws of causality and of freedom as were human beings.

What then are we to say of the Stoic coloring of the sixth book? In the first place, it is not actually Stoic. It is a syncretism of mystical beliefs, developed by Orphic and Apocalyptic poets and mystics from Pythagoras and Plato to a group of Hellenistic writers, popularized by the later less logical Stoic philosophers like Posidonius, and gaining in Vergil's day a wide acceptance among those who were growing impatient of the exacting metaphysical processes of thought. Indeed Vergil contributed something toward foisting these beliefs upon early Christianity, though they were no more essential to it than to Stoicism.

Be that as it may, this mystical setting was here adopted because the poet needed for his own purposes [8] a vision of incorporated souls of Roman heroes, a thing which neither Epicurean nor orthodox Stoic creed could provide. So he created this *mythos* as Plato for his own purpose created a vision of Er.[9] The dramatic purpose of the *descensus* was of course to complete for Aeneas the progressive revelation of his mission, so skilfully developed by

[8] No one would attempt to infer Stephen Phillips' eschatology from the setting of his *Christ in Hades*.

[9] Vergil indeed was careful to warn the reader (VI, 893) that the portal of unreal dreams refers the imagery of the sixth book to fiction, and Servius reiterates the warning. On the employment of myths by Epicureans see chapter VIII, above.

careful stages all through the third book,[10] to give
the hero his final commands and to inspire him for
the final struggle.[11]   Then the poet realized that he
could at the same time produce a powerful artistic
effect upon the reader if he accomplished this by
means of a vision of Rome's great heroes presented
in review by Anchises from the mount of revelations, for this was an age in which Rome was growing proud of her history.   But to do this he must
have a *mythos* which assumed that souls lived before their earthly existence.   A Homeric limbo of
departed souls did not suffice (though Vergil also
availed himself of that in order to recall the friends
of the early books).   With this in view he builds
his home of the dead out of what Servius calls much
sapientia, filling in details here and there even from
the legendary lower-world personages so that the
reader may meet some familiar faces.   However,
the setting is not to be taken literally, for of course
neither he nor anyone else actually believed that
prenatal spirits bore the attributes and garments of
their future existence.   Nor is the poet concerned
about the eschatology which had to be assumed for
the setting; but his judgments on life, though
afforded an opportunity to find expression through

[10] See Heinze, *Epische Technik*, pp. 82 ff.
[11] This Vergil indicates repeatedly: *Aen.* V, 737; VI, 718,
806-7, 890-2.

the characters of the scene, are not allowed to be circumscribed by them; they are his own deepest convictions.

It has frequently been said that Vergil's philosophical system is confused and that his judgments on providence are inconsistent, that in fact he seems not to have thought his problems through. This is of course true so far as it is true of all the students of philosophy of his day. Indeed we must admit that with the very inadequate psychology of that time no reasonable solution of the then central problem of determinism could be found. But there is no reason for supposing that the poet did not have a complete mastery of what the best teachers of his day had to offer.

Vergil's Epicureanism, however, served him chiefly as a working hypothesis for scientific purposes. With its ethical and religious implications he had not concerned himself; and so it was not permitted in his later days to interfere with a deep respect for the essentials of religion. Similarly, the profoundest students of science today, men who in all their experiments act implicitly and undeviatingly on the hypotheses of atomism and determinism in the world of research, are usually the last to deny the validity of the basic religious tenets. In his knowledge of religious rites Vergil reveals an exact-

ness that seems to point to very careful observances
in his childhood home.   They have become second
nature as it were, and go as deep as the filial devotion which so constantly brings the word *pietas* to his
pen.

But his religion is more than a matter of rites and
ceremonies.   It has, to a degree very unusual for
a Roman, associated itself with morality and
especially with social morality.   The culprits of his
Tartarus are not merely the legendary offenders
against exacting deities:

> Hic quibus invisi fratres, dum vita manebat,
> Pulsatusve parens et fraus innexa clienti,
> Aut qui divitiis soli incubuere repertis
> Nec partem posuere suis, quae maxima turba est.

The virtues that win a place in Elysium indicate the
same fusion of religion with humanitarian sympathies:

> Hic manus ob patriam pugnando vulnera passi,
> Quique sacerdotes casti, dum vita manebat,
> Quique pii vates et Phoebo digna locuti,
> Inventas aut qui vitam excoluere per artis,
> Quique sui memores aliquos fecere merendo:
> Omnibus his nivea cinguntur tempora vitta.

His Elysium is far removed from Homer's limbo;
truly did he deserve his place among those

> Phoebo digna locuti.

Before he had completed his work the poet set out for Greece to visit the places which he had described and which in his fastidious zeal he seems to have thought in need of the same careful examination that he had accorded his Italian scenery. Three years he still thought requisite for the completion of his epic. But at Megara he fell ill, and being carried back in Augustus' company to Brundisium he died there, in 19 B. C. at the age of fifty-one. Before his death he gave instructions that his epic should be burned and that his executors, his life-long friends Varius and Tucca, should suppress whatever of his manuscripts he had himself failed to publish. In order to save the *Aeneid*, however, Augustus interposed the supreme authority of the state to annul that clause of the will. The minor works were probably left unpublished for some time. Indeed, there is no convincing proof that such works as the *Ciris*, the *Aetna*, and the *Catalepton* were circulated in the Augustan age.

The ashes were carried to his home at Naples and buried beneath a tombstone bearing the simple epitaph written by some friend who knew the poet's simplicity of heart:

Mantua me genuit, Calabri rapuere, tenet nunc
Parthenope; cecini pascua rura duces.

His tomb [12] was on the roadside outside the city, as was usual — Donatus says on the highway to Puteoli, nearly two miles from the gates. Recent examination of the region has shown that by some cataclysm of the middle ages not mentioned in any record, the road and the tomb have subsided, and now the quiet waters of the golden bay flow many fathoms over them.

[12] Günther, *Pausilypon*, p. 201.

INDEX

INDEX

Acestes, 74.

Aeneas, 174–7.

Aeneid, the, 43, 45, 55, 70, 72, 75, 76, 167–194.

Aetna, the, 58–63, 65, 98, 102.

Alexandrian poetry, 53, 138, 146, 168 ff.

Alfenus Varus, 14, 123, ff.

Allegory, 110 ff., 129.

Ancestry of Vergil, 4.

Animism, 162.

Annius Cimber, 81.

Antiquarian lore in the *Aeneid*, 171.

Antony, Mark, 18, 46, 78 ff., 81 ff.

Antony, Lucius, at Perugia, 124.

Apollodorus, the rhetorician, 19, 145, 148.

Apollonius of Rhodes, 44, 178.

Archias, the poet, 57.

Asianists, the, 18.

Atticists, the, 19, 66, 86, 118, 150.

Auctor ad Herennium, 21.

Augustus, 176; cf. Octavius.

Avernus, Lake, 57.

Birt's edition of the *Catalepton*, 20, 24.

Brutus, M. Junius, 35, 78, 87 ff., 141.

Bucolics, the, see *Eclogues*.

Burial-place of Vergil, 194.

Caecilius of Caleacte, 56.

Callimachus, 38, 130.

Calvus, C. Licinius, 19, 43.

Capua, 130.

Cassius, Longinus, C., 51, 77, 87 ff.

Catalepton, No. I, 52, 65; II, 85; III, 25; IV, 65; V, 20, 47, 48; VII, 52, 53; VIII, 7, 95; IX, 68, 89–96; X, 81 ff.; XIII, 23, 24; XIV, 67, 69.

Catullus, C. Valerius, 14, 37–40, 42–45, 53, 65, 80, 81 ff., 93, 139, 146–9, 169.

Celts, the, 5 ff.

Child, of the fourth *Eclogue*, 137.

Cicero, M. *T*ullius, 19, 20, 49, 78 ff., 132, 139.

Cinna, C. Helvius, 14, 43, 117, 132.

Ciris, the, 26, 35–47, 87 ff., 96, 99, 146, 169, 170.

Cisalpine Gaul, 13.

Civil War, the, 22.

Classicism, 140 ff., 145–151.

Cleopatra and Dido, 75.